THE
FAROE
ISLANDS

THE
FAROE
ISLANDS

A Travel Guide for Sport Fisher

Mauritia Kirchner

Great care was taken when compiling these texts and pictures. Despite this, it is impossible to completely eliminate the possibility of error. The publisher, author and editor do not accept any legal or general liability for erroneous information or any consequences deriving thereof.

All rights are reserved, including rights over photomechanical reproduction and storage on electronic media. Commercial use of the work contained in this product is prohibited.

Editor: Kim Solveig May
Cover design and all picture rights (unless indicated otherwise): Mauritia Kirchner

Imprint
Copyright: © 2024 Mauritia Kirchner, www.mauritiakirchner.com

Print: FlyerAlarm, Würzburg and/or KDP
ISBN 978-3-00-045107-2

For my family, who have unswervingly supported me and showed understanding for all my undertakings.

About the author

There are those who fish to prove themselves.
There are those who fish to prove themselves but who would never admit that for social reasons.
Then there are those who fish.
I count myself amongst the latter.

Fishing has fascinated me ever since I was a child, both from a sporting as well as from a biological perspective. I approach animals, nature and culture with the greatest respect and understanding.

My professional life has also been shaped by cultural inquisitiveness.
25 years with the German airline Lufthansa took me all around the world to countless exotic locations. Ten further years as a businesswoman running a studio for the reproduction of historic clothing took me deep into European history.

Despite this, there is hardly a profession that furnishes one with so many stories as fishing – from the high seas to wispy rivulets, from rich to poor, from "mate" to "His Royal Majesty" and sadly also from life to death, on, by and in the water. I have come to know them and have made it my task to tell their stories – because we are all fishermen.

For more information see: mauritiakirchner.com

Contents

Chapter 1

About the Faroe Islands

Heard of them but not quite sure where they are? That's how it is with most people so.

Page:

1. Geographic Location
2. The Faroe Islands
3. Geology
4. Climate
5. Fauna
6. Flora
7. History
8. The Faroese People
9. Language
10. Government
11. Income
12. Currency
13. Infrastructure
14. Religion
15. The Sea and its Victims
16. Traditions
17. Food
18. Art
19. Sport
20. Music

Contents

Chapter 2

Planning the Journey: Heading North!

It's easier than you might think – and a warm welcome awaits you!

Page:

27. With Your Own Car
28. By Ferry
29. By Air
30. Import Regulations
31. Tourist Information Offices
32. Hotels
33. Youth Hostels
34. Campsites
35. Holiday Homes
36. Choosing a Location
37. Useful Information

Contents

Chapter 3

The Strike of Thor´s Hammer

The Capital Tórshavn:
"And though it be but little..."

Page:

41. Restaurants
42. Bar Food
43. Pubs
44. Nightlife
45. Fishing Stores
46. Shopping
47. Food
48. Alcohol
49. Culture
50. Souvenirs
51. Harbour
52. Walks
53. Markets
54. Useful Information

Contents

Chapter 4

"Who is Who" on the Faroe Islands

Freshwater Fishing: the Big Three on the Faroe Islands.
Nowhere else to be found so close together.

Page:

59. Occurrence
60. Salmon
61. Sea Trout
62. Brown Trout
63. Char

Saltwater Fishing: From Cod to Pink Salmon
Nowhere else in such numbers at sea.

64. Pink Salmon
65. Steelhead and Flat Fish
66. Cod from the pier
67. Cod, Ling, Haddock, Pollack, etc.

Contents

Chapter 5

Tight Lines!

There are no guarantees that you'll catch a lot of fish, but armed with these tips you'll increase your chances.

Page:

71. Waters
72. Time of Travel
73. Fishing Regulations
74. Catch & Release
75. Prey animals
76. Clothing
77. Fly Fishing Equipment
78. Flies
79. Tips for fishermen

Contents

Chapter 6

Fishing on Streymoy, the Isle of Many Faces

Prepare to be amazed!

Page:

85. Map of Streymoy
86. Tjørnuvík
87. Saksun Fjord
88. Saksun Pollur
89. Saksun Lake
90. Nesvik
91. Rivers
92. Hvalvik Stora
93. Vestmanna Lakes
94. Vestmanna Harbour
95. Leynar Beach
96. Fish Ladder
97. Leynarvatn
98. Mjáuvøtn
99. Kollafjørður
100. Kalbaksbotnur
101. Argir
102. Sightseeing Tips

Contents

Chapter 7

Fishing on Eysturoy, the Majestic Isle

Mysterious and formidable – just like the waters!

Page:

109. Map of Eysturoy
110. The Dammed Lake of Eiði
109. The Bay of Malarvegur
110. Skálabotnur
111. Toftavatn
112. Saithe in Leirvik
113. Sightseeing Tips

Contents

Chapter 8

Fishing on Sandoy, the Sweet and Gentle Isle

The weather's like Ibiza – but here it's the fishermen who party!

Page:

121. Map of Sandoy
122. Real Estate Poker
123. Pier Fishing in Skopun
124. Norđara Halsavatn
125. Sandsvatn
126. Sandsvágur
127. Storavatn
128. Litlavatn
129. Sightseeing Tips

Contents

Chapter 9

Fishing on Suðuroy, the Wild Isle

Pirate cliffs, Saracens, Vikings – which way is the wind blowing?

Page:

135. Map of Suðuroy
136. Hvalba
137. Nesvegur/Hvalba
138. Trongisvágur
139. Øravik
140. Fámjin
141. Sightseeing Tips

Contents

Chapter 10

Fishing on Vágar, the Nondescript Isle

Unspectacular only at first glance!

Page:

147. Map of Vágar
148. Leitisvatn
149. Fjallavatn
150. Sightseeing Tips

Chapter 11

Ship Ahoy!

On the high seas, where men are still men.

Page:

159. Skipper
160. Side Note: Not all that flutters is fish

Contents

Chapter 12

Faroese Food Culture

Or how to survive in the North Atlantic.

Page

164. to 169.

Contents

Chapter 13

The Pilot Whale Hunt or „Grindadráp"

A controversial topic.

Page:

172. and 173.

SUMMARY

Sport Fishing on the Faroe Islands

Page:

177. to 180.

Chapter 1

About the Faroe Islands

The Faroe Islands – heard of them but not quite sure where they are? That's how it is with most people.

It is said that God, on the seventh day, exhausted after having finished creating the world, scraped out the dirt from under his fingernails. What fell to earth became the Faroe Islands. Does that all sound a bit too theological for you? If so, a rather more historical legend claims that the Vikings had a small problem as they set off towards the northwest: seasick sailors. The rocks upon which the "ballast" was unceremoniously left later became known as the Faroe Islands.

Whatever really happened, when you arrive on the Faroe Islands you'll be amazed at what a population of around 53,000 has managed to put together right in the middle of the harshness of the North Atlantic.
Or perhaps you already knew that a town the size of Lancaster is able to administer an area of 540 square miles, including its own parliament and gross domestic product of £1.2 billion, its own language, currency, universities, airline, stamps, a TV channel and three radio stations – not to mention the football team, which may well be the reason why the name "Faroe Islands" rings a bell for you. By the way, all the residents of the Faroe Islands would fit into Newcastle's St James' Park stadium with room to spare.

Answer honestly: aren't there enough travel destinations about which you've heard too much, and of which you already have far too many pictures in your head? Tradition survives on the Faroe Islands, and has done for over 1,000 years. The cooperation between people, and between man and nature, has hardly changed over that time; roving Saracens, evangelising Danes and tourists and journalists looking for the last remaining paradise aside. It's no surprise that the Faroe Islands are regular named by National Geographic Traveller as the Number 1 Island Paradise – even though the sheep-rearing island was running in competition against palm-studded idylls and coral reefs. This book was written to explain why.

Ideal location in the fish-rich North Atlantic

62° North.
The Faroe Islands lie on this latitude, which is often used by young agencies as an advertising slogan. The Faroe Islands share the 62° latitude with Alaska, Yukon in Canada, Greenland's southern peninsula and the northern regions of Norway, Sweden and Finland. However, thanks to the Gulf Stream, which blesses this country with rich fishing grounds, it doesn't get nearly as cold here. The location also makes the Faroe Islands special in another regard: the Faroese people have their own enduring identity and were, after centuries of persistence, finally recognised as an independent state – more or less – in 1948. They stand under the protectorate of Denmark. The Faroe Islands are not a member of the EU and, as a result, entry requirements and import regulations are the same as other non-EU countries. Nevertheless, Greenland, Iceland, the Faroe Islands, Norway, Finland, Sweden and Denmark have formed an alliance that guarantees the citizens of these countries extended rights of movement when choosing their place of residence and work. This is, however, little consolation for any "southerners" wishing to move northwards.

....concentrated on 18 islands!

The view from the window.
Wind from the north.
Fishing in Leynar today? Or low waves at the beaches: the wind takes the line far out to sea...

Fishing on the Faroe Islands is as easy as ABC and is as intuitive as riding a bike. No point is further than 5km from water.
As a result, the 18 islands offer numerous options for the indefatigable fisherman. You can choose between fishing on the open sea, from a mole, on the beach or in one of the many lakes. Simply stick your finger in the air, determine the wind direction, read the weather from the sky – or load a detailed weather analysis onto your iPhone – and you'll soon find the ideal spot on the Faroe Islands for the day.

On top of it all: a spot of geography

The Faroe Islands can, essentially, be imagined as a mountain range whose peaks protrude up out of the sea. That's how steep and dramatic the Faroese landscape is, in places dropping down 882 metres into the sea. As a rule, the rivers are only small rivulets which dry up after periods without rain. After heavy rain, in contrast, impressive waterfalls form all over the place. Here's a nugget of information which always impresses in conversation: although the Faroe Islands are volcanic in origin, they have the glaciers to thank for the way they look today. These glaciers formed and moved over the Faroe Islands in the Quaternary period, leaving magnificent basins for small lakes in the process. Thanks be to God!

Here is a chart listing the expressions most often used by people visiting the Faroe Islands for the first time:
No. 1: Oh, it's just like being in Lord of the Rings...
No. 2: It looks a lot like New Zealand... (Note: that's where they filmed Lord of the Rings) No. 3: It's like Iceland – only smaller
No. 4: It looks like Lesotho (Note: it's difficult to verify the accuracy of this statement) No. 5: The most beautiful place I have ever seen (Elton John)
No. 6: These grass roofs are a great idea; I'll try it on my holiday house (Bill Clinton)

Dream weather: the source of countless low-pressure areas

Even its climate makes the Faroe Islands the ideal country for fishing. The Gulf Stream makes for relatively mild winters (3°C on average) and the northerly location ensures fresh, windy summers (11°C on average). It is light 24 hours a day around midsummer in June – meaning 24 hours of fishing pleasure for those who have the stamina for it. And the wind takes care of the rest. A stiff breeze helps those who lack casting experience so that even beginners can feel like nonchalant professionals every once in a while.

However, caution is advised. The Faroe Islands are very different from your Alpine lakes and idyllic ponds. The climate is rough, the natural landscape archaic and life with the elements of earth and water is direct and immediate. You have to be respectful and that means, quite simply, being prepared for anything. If the sun is shining at 10am, you're often glad to have brought a raincoat by 11am. The canny Faroese even have a quick look at the webcams on the internet showing live footage of their destination before setting off on a trip. It is not unusual for the sun to be shining in Tórshavn while it's pouring down with rain 17 miles further on because a raincloud is stranded between two mountains.

> The phenomenon of water flowing skywards is a common sight and can often be observed on the Faroe Islands: strong winds push the waterfalls upwards.
> Recommended weather websites: www.yr.no or www.landsverk.fo

Native inhabitants, settlers, tourists: the animal kingdom

As with the human population, a distinction can also be made in the animal kingdom between those who have always been on the Faroe Islands, those who settled there later (or were brought there) and those who pop by every once in a while. Technically speaking, animals are the real native inhabitants of the islands. Those travelling by ferry encounter their first species on board the Norröna. The smyril – or merlin, a bird of prey – is emblazoned on the ship's enormous chimney. Like some other birds, such as the oystercatcher or some types of starlings, it leads a quiet life due to the fact that it's not to be found on the plates of humans. Its close relatives the puffin and the fulmar, likewise native inhabitants of the islands, glance enviously at the merlin from the cooking pot. That countless populations of seabirds can occasionally be observed here is due to the fact that the Faroe Islands serve as a stopping point on their migration routes and as nesting grounds for many species. Interestingly, the animal population usually associated with the Faroe Islands (sheep, ponies and freshwater fish such as the brown trout) were first introduced and cultivated by man. The same is true of rats, mice and wasps, all of which knew how to make the best use of the advantages of modern shipping.

> By the way, although they were first brought to the islands by humans, many species have remained genetically pure due to the Faroe Islands' isolated location – the greylag goose, the brown trout and the Faroese pony, for example.

Barren landscapes: the pros and cons

Pros: isn't it obvious? For fly fishermen, barren landscapes mean full fly boxes! No trees, no shrubs, no natural obstacles for the fly to get caught up in. Because of the wind, the sheep and the lack of saltwater, it's tough for trees to take root. But "barren" is by no means the same as "boring", and certainly not the same as "bleak". The eye is drawn to fascinating moor landscapes, aromatic herbs and bizarre mosses and lichens. In June, all the meadows are abloom with marsh marigolds and the Faroese lady's mantle, Alchemilla faeroensis.

Cons: there is hardly any arable farming on the Faroe Islands. In the past it took some effort to wring some hay out of the earth for the sheep, along with some rhubarb, turnips and, later, potatoes. Today, it still resembles a defiant ritual when a Faroese tills the soil in spring on a small patch in his garden to plant potatoes there for a small harvest in autumn. After the work is finished, pictures are proudly displayed on Facebook and when the first guests are invited to a meal of potatoes, the precious items are counted exactly to ensure that they're fairly distributed between all the plates. And rightly so: the potatoes that arrive here after a long sea voyage can hardly compete with theirs, in terms of taste or appearance.

Native inhabitants, settlers, tourists: the animal kingdom

Once the glaciers had melted and microorganisms, plants and seeds from Scandinavia and Scotland had made the scree landscape green, the islands plodded along quietly for the first few hundred thousand years. The first time that humans set foot on the islands was in AD 600, when Irish monks arrived. They were followed by the wanderlusty Vikings, who, during the course of the next centuries, established well-organised and functioning social structures, including a surprisingly modern judiciary, called the "thing", the site of which can still be seen today. They also left behind countless legends, stories and myths of courageous heroes. But then more outsiders arrived and with them came Christianity and a new administration. In this case it was the Norwegians and the Danes who put an end to Faroese independence in the Middle Ages. It wasn't until the nineteenth century that new impulses for rediscovering their distinct identity arose, such as by writing down the Faroese language for the first time. The national flag was invented by Faroese students in 1919. One of them had a helpful big sister who sewed the first prototypes. After the end of the Second World War the Faroe Islands were recognised as an autonomous state.

> Recent gene research has revealed some juicy information: according to the analysis, Faroese men are largely descended from the Vikings, while Faroese women predominantly carry Celtic genes. That leads to the inference that there was a lack of women among seafarers, resulting in indiscriminate sourcing measures being taken in neighbouring countries...

The Little Book of Etiquette: Don't do a Paul Watson!

A deeply rooted part of the Faroese culture is the battle against nature for food. Food is in short supply. The way the Faroese saw things, if anything on the islands was in danger of extinction, then it was man, not the food.
But man has succeeded in mastering life in this formidable natural landscape using willpower, courage, stamina, diligence, education and powerful social bonds. No sustenance ever falls into man's lap, as is the case in other more temperate climes. In gratitude and with a sense of responsibility for his handling of the resources at hand, man has taken the gifts of the sea and still behaves to this day in a conscious and sustainable manner – even when Paul Watson comes to visit.
If you know of the controversial environmental activist and whale protector and his aggressive communication methods, you can well imagine the clash of ideologies that occurred. To begin with, the Faroese were astonished at the boats, helicopters and cameras used for monitoring and escorting the islanders in their own waters. They received the activists with equanimity and humour at the harbour, offering a cold buffet with national dishes (whale, fulmar, lamb).

Do you speak Viking?

To put it simply, the Faroese language is that of the Vikings. However, it has also naturally evolved and is now a distinct Nordic language spoken only here by the 48,000 residents. Until the eighteenth and nineteenth centuries, it was only passed down orally and it was a huge pioneering feat by a number of scholars to render it in writing. The similarities between German and Faroese vocabulary and grammar are often proudly pointed out to visitors. During the course of the last few centuries Danish was the official language and it is still used in parallel with Faroese in a number of domains. Every child learns Danish from an early age, not least because many school textbooks are Danish. It's not unusual for school-leavers to head for Denmark to begin their studies. Faroese sounds harmonious and melodic and is pronounced completely differently to the way it is written. Time and again it is surprising how the place names Tórshavn, Kirkjubøur or Kollafjørður change aurally and that the beer "Gull" sounds more like a famous search engine. Tourists, however, get along fine with English – whether talking to schoolchildren or shepherds, the standard of English spoken is so high that it often puts us to shame.

Tip: How about learning Faroese?
The University in Tórshavn offers a course every summer.

How independent is independent?

"Nation within the Danish Realm" is the official status of the Faroe Islands. It is unclear whether the Faroe Islands will ever be a state with 100% independence. It is also unclear whether this is even a worthwhile aim. There are two sides to every coin. On the one side, certain things such as a global financial system or their own military can surely not be achieved by such a small country. And in terms of certain day-to-day matters such as food deliveries, the Faroe Islands are completely dependent on Denmark. It is also problematic that Denmark is a member of the EU while the Faroe Islands cannot and will not become a member of the EU so as not to have to share their vital fishing grounds with the rest of the continent. However, just as in other matters, the question regarding the definition and implementation of national status is regarded with true Nordic equanimity. Wait and see, and find an interim solution. The best example of this is the police force. Police officers are selected on the islands, trained in Denmark and then return to the islands to carry out their duty. And if a Faroese were ever to be sent to prison, which rarely happens due to their having the world's lowest crime rate, then they're off to spend time behind Danish bars.

> The white parliament building in Tórshavn city centre houses the parliamentary assembly. Historic buildings that have been used for trade and administration from the earliest times can be seen on a rocky peninsula in the harbour area.
> Tinganes, on the outermost tip, is especially worth seeing.

A life by the sea, in the sea and from the sea

You see them driving around everywhere: heavy trucks laden with huge refrigerated containers filled with fish. They are delivered to and processed everywhere you go on the Faroe Islands – codfish, pollack and haddock, as well as farmed salmon from countless producers in the fjords. The Faroese fishing fleet, almost 200 ships strong, and the captains of the many small one-man cutters bring to land what the 200 nautical miles around the islands or the North Atlantic yields. Fishing alone makes up 95% of the Faroese economic output, whether directly or indirectly. The barkeeper who sells the deck hand a beer, the newspaper publisher, the electrician or the supermarket: they're all dependent on the export of Faroese fish. Paradoxically, there is hardly a supermarket that sells fresh fish here, because why would you buy fish when your brother-in-law or your neighbour works on a longliner and brings round a box every once in a while? At this point we should put an end to one cliché. A country that makes its living from fishing brings to mind pictures of lonely farmsteads, bumpy roads and residents dishevelled by storms. Well, forget that! The Faroe Islands are a modern, dynamic state with high education standards and residents who like to drive down to a bistro in their Porsche Cayennes every now and then, followed by a stroll through the pulsating nightlife of the capital. What's more, they're also thinking about alternatives to fishing. Today, 30% of the Faroe Island's energy is already produced from water or wind power. Oil production is also being discussed. And last but not least, some have their hopes set on tourism, from which every guest in this country benefits hugely.

Money, money, money – or: the first catch!

Faroese money is beautiful, and perhaps especially so for fishermen. Watercolours by the Faroese artist Zacharias Heinesen decorate the banknotes on one side, while drawings of native animals can be seen on the reverse side, amongst them, of course, members of the sea kingdom. The Faroe Islands have their own notes, but they use Danish coins. The total amount of money in circulation is equal to the gross national product – a clever budgetary policy, no doubt. That being said, the island paradise was not spared from a massive financial crisis at the end of the 1980s and the beginning of the 1990s. Some lost house and home, while some had to take on the debts of their children against possessions that had been in the family for centuries. Many emigrated to Denmark to begin a new life there. Most, however, have returned in the meantime.

> You can, of course, use your bank card to withdraw money at cash machines or to pay (using your PIN) at most shops, restaurants and petrol stations. It is, however, always advisable to have other credit cards at hand. VISA is the one most widely used here but you'll also get along fine with a MasterCard.
> Tip: you should also have the PIN number of your credit card at the ready.

On the open road

Before you pack up your 4x4 with fuel canisters, spades and a ladder and head off towards what are assumed to be off-road routes, rest assured that the infrastructure of the Faroe Islands is exemplary and is suitable for all kinds of vehicles, from Minis to people-carriers. Modern buses travel many times a day along well-maintained roads between all villages; ferries meeting the highest safety standards travel between islands that have no direct access. Where there is no ferry, Atlantic Airways flies schoolchildren, foodstuffs or pub-goers using helicopters (booked in advance and with a minimum stay of one day, of course) from the remote islands, usually to Tórshavn. Not bad! Where once only rowing boats linked the settlements, the Faroese have spent the last few decades digging like voles through the mountains, building tunnels for essential links – which played an important part in maintaining the population of the more remote villages. At the beginning of the 1960s, the first underpasses were built, which were single lane to begin with. From the beginning of the 1980s, the first modern, two-lane tunnels were built and at the beginning of the twenty-first century, the first underground connections below the Atlantic opened, connecting the island of Streymoy, Vágar, Eysturoy, Sandoy, and Borðoy.

Bus and ferry connections at: www.ssl.fo

Every now and then the driver will come into contact with the old single-lane tunnels (hopefully not). Great concentration is required because in one direction you always have to give way to oncoming traffic.

Religion: a cross that everyone carries

Put yourself in this situation: you have a husband and two sons. Both are sailing the high seas on unsound boats, working to earn a living for the family. No-one can foresee if and when a storm will be coming – or where. Wouldn't you, as a woman, go to pray for their safe return in one of the churches built close to the coast? Religion plays an important part in the lives of the Faroese for exactly this reason. The wooden churches that are characteristic of the Faroe Islands reflect much of this difficult burden. The older Faroese fishermen's refusal to go fishing on Sundays is also understandable in this context. As is so often the case, religion also has a political, business and social dark side. In former times, parishes were led by Danish priests – the easiest and most effective opportunity to exert Danish influence. More than 80% of the Faroese population belong to the Protestant-Lutheran denomination and slightly more than 10% describe themselves as Ebenezer, followers of William Gibson Sloan, who undertake a lot of missionary work. It used to be the case that the awarding of contracts and jobs was heavily influenced by one's religious affiliation. One can still see the influence of religion in day-to-day life, for instance in the restriction of alcohol sales and the rarity of homosexual relationships. Nevertheless, with divorce and self-assured single mothers, the Faroese have arrived in the twenty-first century. See, it is possible!

> Don't miss out on a visit to Kirkjubøur the spiritual and cultural centre of the Faroe Islands from the very beginning. It is on the UNESCO World Heritage Site candidature list.

The sea and its victims

The ocean yields riches. But when it takes back, it demands infinitely more. To this day ships set off to sea with only a promise – not a guarantee – that they'll bring the men and the boys home safely. In the past, storms and shipwrecks could wipe out the working male population of whole villages, forcing women and children to give up their settlement and move away. If you'd like to get to know this side of the Faroe Islands too – and it moves the heart of every real fisherman – the best tip is to listen to the country's stories. In almost every town and village you'll find memorials and gravestones with the names of men and boys who were virtually still children when they died at sea. Take a seat in "Glitnir", a sailors' pub in the harbour area in Tórshavn, buy a round of beer and listen to the stories of the "stormy, stormy weather". A particularly tragic chapter played out in the nineteenth century when the English sold their disused ships to the Faroese. The era of steamships had arrived for the Royal Navy. The Faroese could not take such financial leaps and used these sailing boats to go fishing – entirely unsuitable for this purpose. It cost many men their lives. Having said that, the Faroese, as descendants of the Vikings, are regarded as the best sailors in the world with a finely tuned sense for safety and practically no readiness for risk. But their sea is malevolent: the sudden changes in the weather, strong tides and powerful currents are deadly. Not for nothing are the Faroe Islands also called "the land of maybe": you never know whether you'll be able to go out to sea the following day. Here, everything is done in accordance with the weather and you are well advised to pay more heed to what the Faroese tell you than to the weather reports when it comes to plans to venture outdoors.

Traditions and culture: don't expect a theme park

Yes, we have culture. No, we don't commercialise it. That's a summary of where the Faroese stand on the conflict between culture and tourism. After all, the country was voted Number 1 in the world by National Geographic Traveller not just for its untouched natural landscapes but also because of its culture. Traditions are practised quietly and naturally during family celebrations and on the national holiday. Take the famous chain dance, for example. Without it and the ballads sung with it, the Faroese language would not have survived. It is regarded today as the only one of its kind in the world.

Their dress is also extraordinary: they wear the red or black caps, which are reminiscent of the seafarers' hats of the seventeenth and eighteenth centuries, with their heads held high. You'll also see the traditional, finely embroidered costumes worn by high-school leavers and, of course, bridal couples or their guests. Each member of the Faroese population makes a contribution to the culture in their own individual way – in terms of art, music and craftsmanship. The so-called "Grindadráp" is a very controversial topic in Faroese culture (see chapter 13).

> If you can, take your holiday during the national holiday, St Olaf's Day (Ólavsøka), which takes place at the end of July each year. You won't regret it!

Faroese Cuisine: a taste for survival

Don't worry: these days on the Faroe Islands you are, of course, on familiar culinary territory, even if most offerings outside of Tórshavn leave a little to be desired. In contrast, the capital has something to please every palate, from an Irish Pub to a star chef, who, by the way, is the best friend of the head chef of the "Noma" in Copenhagen. It was different back in the day. You had to eat whatever the air, water and land gave you. Puffins, fulmars, guillemots and their eggs. Fish prepared in every possible way, usually boiled or dried. Pilot whale meat and mutton. They'd already realised in the thirteenth century that the islands would not be able to support more than 70,000 sheep. And since this was not enough for the human population, making use of the pilot whale was clearly necessary for survival. Fish was the main meal and would be eaten up to five times a week. To this day, meat is still dried in the drying houses, one of which stands next to almost every Faroese home. Beyond that there was practically nothing. The harvests of rhubarb, turnips and, later, potatoes were meagre. The Faroese women skilfully baked and prepared everything they had at their disposal, and were adept in the kitchen and at knitting. They used to make a distinction between the portions for the hard-working men and those for the women. That might be described as privation – but it doesn't appear to be unhealthy to live off what nature provides. In any case, the elderly Faroese look not dissimilar to the hundred-year-old Japanese who only eat fish all their lives. For more on Faroese cuisine on the crossroad between Michelin stars and dried fish, read chapter 12.

Art – first find it, then foster it

"If we have a talent – we'll find it." That's what the manager of the Faroe Islands' national football team once said. This statement can be easily carried over to the realm of culture too. That this small nation produces so many artists is thanks to the fact that Faroese talents are not only discovered, but are also given a lot of support. The Faroese public takes pride in their culture, they delight in each contribution and they show due respect and attention to the work that is produced.

Most works are, of course, strongly influenced by the spectacular landscape. You'll find paintings that have this as their theme in every home. The city is also a gallery in its own right: there is hardly a corner or a square in Tórshavn that is not adorned by a sculpture.

William Heinesen (1900–1991) should be named here as THE Faroese artist of the twentieth century. He was a universal genius and he left an amazing legacy that includes both literary as well as artistic work.

> Tórshavn has an excellent art museum, the Listasavn Føroya in Gundadalsvegur 9
> It's well worth a visit!

Goaaaaaaaal! But that's not all...

If you want to shake Ronaldo´s hand or trip up Manuel Neuer in goal, before going back to the grandstand to drink a beer with Faroese fans and to rue each goal in the European Championship, then you've come to the right place: the stadium of Tórshavn. As you can imagine, Faroese stadiums are small and are little more than parks, and yet the stars of the football world come here to compete on the international stage. Of course, the Faroe Islands had to comply with FIFA regulations first – floodlights higher than most houses, cans of hairspray for the Italian teams. Yet despite this, most visiting teams are reluctant to come here. Why is that? Is it the weather? Or perhaps because the Faroese team, which actually never really expects to win and consists almost completely of amateurs, is only allowed to play as a national team and as a result fights like a hoard of lions for a win?

Yet football is not the only thing that counts on the island. The dominant national sport is rowing – they are, after all, a society that lives in close proximity to water. Almost every area has its own rowing teams which can often be seen training in the fjords. The annual championships take place in Tórshavn on St Olaf's Day (Ólavsøka).

In 1986, Ove Joensen from the island of Nólsoy even rowed his Faroese boat in 41 days from his island to Copenhagen, where he received a frenzied welcome. He sadly drowned a year later after falling from his boat. It is thought that he had been making merry in Tórshavn.

> B36 and HB Tórshavn are the two football teams in Tórshavn.
> Make a note of it for pub conversations!

Music: One hell of a show

One hardly dares to say it, but when it comes to song the Faroese exceed the cliché of the jovial Scandinavian, be that while singing the ballads of the chain dance, while singing loudly during celebrations, or – naturally – at midnight on Ólavsøka, when thousands of people join in together.

But their musical tradition is also successfully exported: many of the country's best musicians are international stars. Teitur, Bandur Enni, Eivør Pálsdóttir and Guðrið Hansdóttir, and rock bands such as Týr or Gestir are known beyond the country's borders.

In the capital's cultural centre, the Nordic House (Faroese: Norðurlandahúsið) in Tórshavn, concerts are regularly held by the National Symphony Orchestra, local musicians and visiting artists from abroad.

A great show awaits you at the festivals that take place annually on the Faroe Islands. The G! Festival in Gøta is even considered to be one of the best in Europe. The weather is perhaps not always helpful, but on the Faroe Islands that is no reason not to party.

A short anecdote: when Bonnie Tyler was supposed to appear at a festival on the island of Sandoy, none of her suitcases had arrived with her. Without further ado, she bought herself a new set of clothes and by the time she was on stage she'd put it all behind her. She even claimed that she'd never seen such beautiful women as she'd seen here.

So, gentlemen: off to the G! Festival!

Chapter 2

Planning the Journey: Heading North!

It's easier than you might think – and a warm welcome awaits you!

Admittedly, people don't usually decide on the spur of the moment to spend their holidays on the Shetlands, the Orkneys, the Hebrides or on the Faroe Islands. But these destinations are no longer on the other side of the world.

The Faroe Islands are becoming an increasingly popular travel destination – although it must be said that until a few years ago only a few visitors to the Faroe Islands were holidaymakers in the truest sense of the word. Most visitors were Danes or Faroese visiting relatives for a couple of weeks, or business travellers, or are just passing through on their way to the larger neighbour, Iceland.

In the meantime, the rest of the world has also become aware of the archipelago and the number of tourists who travel following an insider tip specifically to the unspoiled islands and are standing at the cliffs, overwhelmed by the spectacular landscape, is increasing from year to year.

But still, when you go to the Faroe Islands as a tourist and have consciously chosen to spend your holidays in this country you will encounter the locals with its propensity for helpfulness, patience and tolerance. You won't fall victim to the great tourist rip-off on these islands – the Faroese are simply not wired like that.

The capacity of hotel beds was previously so small that a smaller travel group could occupy an entire hotel, but large hotel chains have also responded to the increasing demand and built two large additional hotel complexes in Tórshavn in no time.

Not that you won't be able to find a room today – careful planning is nevertheless the key to a carefree night's sleep.

You'll find professional assistance everywhere you go: each one of the major islands has its own tourist information office. Incidentally, the central tourism authority is run by a Faroese woman who succeeded in doubling the number of visitors to Stockholm during her time as the head of the tourism authority there. The future's bright!

So, let's head north!

Drive Your Own

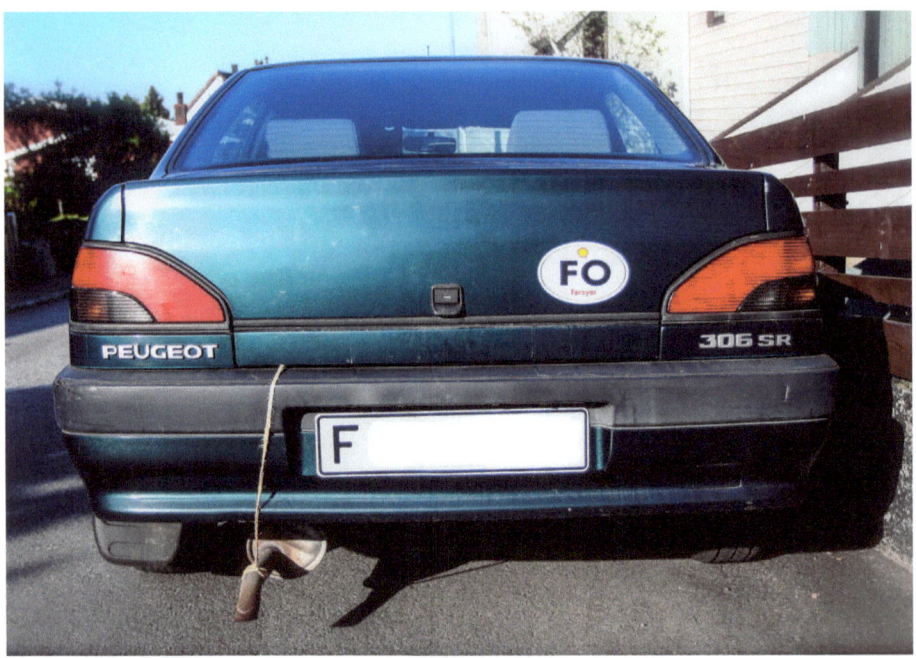

There are only two ways of getting to the Faroe Islands – either by plane with Atlantik Airways the only airline of the Faroe Islands or with SAS.
Or by car and ferry with the only ferry line that goes there.

As a rule of thumb, stays of less than ten days are better undertaken by air. For stays of two weeks or more, it is worth making the journey by ferry. Other factors such as the number of travellers or your amount of luggage will, of course, influence this decision.
Factors that speak for taking your own car include the relatively high price of car rental on the islands, the wonderful ferry crossing (see next page) and, naturally, the special luggage carried by fishermen: the rods can be stowed in the boot, as can all the fish that want to come home with you...

All the car rental companies are listed on the website of the Faroese tourism authority: visitfaroeisalnds.com
Comparing prices is well worth the effort here!

A trip by sea, what fun it can be!

All those taking their cars make the sea crossing on the famous MS Norröna, a vessel that belongs to Smyril Line. In winter she makes the crossing between Denmark and the Faroe Islands once a week, and twice a week in summer. After numerous route changes, she now docks in the Danish port of Hirtshals and no longer makes stopovers in Scotland, on the Shetland Islands or in Bergen, meaning that you arrive on the Faroe Islands after a journey of only 36 hours. By the way, the Norröna is also the only ferry going to Iceland. Therefore it is used by many holidaymakers heading to Iceland, along with their monstrous off-road vehicles. Don't be alarmed! These are not necessary on the Faroe Islands. The Smyril Line, named after the Faroese word for merlin, the only bird of prey resident on the Faroe Islands, was founded in Tórshavn at the beginning of the 1980s. To begin with they only had a small ferry to service its routes, which they'd bought second-hand in Sweden. The Norröna, a combined cargo and passenger ship, was acquired in 2003 and was the final order that a shipbuilder in Lübeck launched. Accomplished Faroese sailors dismissively called her a "shoebox" at first, but soon had to admit that the shoebox not only defied the adversities of the North Atlantic admirably, but on top of everything offered passengers all kinds of entertainment and comfort as if on a real cruise.

> Tickets can be booked online at smyrilline.com
> If you are prone to seasickness, you should take precautions with medication.

In the air: not always a smooth ride...

Just like Smyril Line, the Faroe Islands' only airline, Atlantic Airways, was founded in the 1980s. Considering the limited demand, it is no surprise that Smyril Line and Atlantic Airways have been for many years the only carriers to the islands. All attempts by other providers to break the monopolies have failed due to almost stagnating booking figures.
That has now changed due to the exploding tourist numbers. Both the shipping company and Atlantic Airways are making a profit now. Thanks to the expansion of the runway on the island of Vágar the airline was able to put its first Airbus A319 into operation. Atlantic Airways may be a small airline but it is extremely dynamic. In its ever-evolving network of routes to the European mainland, the most important connections to Copenhagen, Billund and Aalborg remain constant and run three times daily.
Flights to Vágar can at times feel like quite an adventure. When thick fog or clouds have settled over the airport, attempts at flying in can become protracted affairs lasting days, despite the advanced approach system used to improve safety, the RNP AR 0.1, which Atlantic Airways was the first airline in the world to install in its Airbus. Strong winds and thick cloud formations can sometimes make descents a little uncomfortable. The French national football team seems to have been afraid of exactly that. During AVRO times the players said "non" to the journey, insisting that the Faroese team comes to France to play the international match.

Caution when entering and leaving the Faroe Islands!

Entering is a skill to be learned...
Don't take the customs checks when entering the country lightly. The Faroese customs authorities have declared war on smugglers. The very obvious presence of drug detection dogs at airports and seaports is a demonstration of force to incoming passengers. Information about duty-free limits can be found on all of the tourist authority's websites and are also summarised on taks.fo. Fishermen used to be required to have all their fishing equipment disinfected by an official (veterinarian) and to carry documented proof that this had been carried out. There is now no demand for proof but they still appeal to sport fishermen's duty of care. You would hope, however, that approaching the clear, pristine lakes of the Faroe Islands with gyrodactylus would, surely, be unthinkable for any true nature lover in any case.

...and so is leaving
There was no rule limiting the amount of fish that can be taken away from the Faroe Islands. For good reason there is now an export limit of 25kg p.p. And you could be asked when leaving on the ferry how much fish you have with you. It is ok, if it is for private use only. Here too, the principle of honesty is to be observed. As a sport fisherman, it's not likely that you will single-handedly decimate a saltwater fish species. But neither should you develop the ambition of offsetting your travel costs with your haul of fish.

Your diligent little helpers: tourist information offices and websites

The tourist information office in the centre of Tórshavn (Niels Finsens Gøta Nr 17) is usually the first stop for every new arrival.
As an perfect addition, you should visit the oldest shop still in operation on the Faroe Islands and complete your travel literature in this well managed bookshop.
It is well worth a visit! The building was formerly home to the Jakobsen family, the male members of which made an important contribution to the nationalist movement at the end of the nineteenth century. The living quarters of the famous Jakob Jakobsen (1864–1918) are located to the rear of the building and remain unchanged, but they are not open to the public so far.
And if you're shopping for books, don't be surprised if you suddenly find yourself standing next to the Queen of Belgium admiring the unusual shopping bags with their knitted patterns.

Official pages of the tourism authority with all the essential information:
faroeislands.com and visitfaroeislands.com
Pages of the tourist information offices on the individual islands: www.visittorshavn.fo/
www.visitvagar.fo/ www.visiteysturoy.fo/ www.vistisandoy.fo/ www.visitnordoy.fo/
www.visitsuduroy.fo

As one makes his bed, so he must lie

Of course it is to be assumed that wearing waders and carrying your dripping haul of salmon after a hard day's fishing you won't be returning to a four-star hotel. You are almost certain to choose alternative accommodation for a fishing holiday. Nevertheless, a travel guide that makes claims of encyclopaedic completeness cannot omit this chapter.
And in any case, all of Tórshavn's hotels are worth a stay.

Here is a selection of the most common accommodations (a detailed list can be found on the website of the tourist board).

HOTEL FØROYAR is the largest hotel on the Faroe Islands, and its long, flat structure sits high above the capital. From here you can enjoy panoramic views over Tórshavn and the island of Nólsoy. Rooms are often booked as a package in combination with flights or ferry crossings and it serves as the preferred accommodation for all foreign state representatives and sportspeople. It is, however, located far from the town centre.
HOTEL HAFNIA: This is one of the four-star hotels on the island, like the Hotel Føroyar. Located in the town centre it is only half the size of the first.
HOTEL TÓRSHAVN: This three-star hotel and former "sailor's home" comes highly recommended, not least because of its central location by the harbour. What's more, it has a popular bar and brasserie.
HOTEL BRANDAN: Opening of this hotel was in 2020. It is part of the Smyril Line / Hotel Hafnia company.
HOTEL HILTON GARDEN INN: Even the Hilton Group has not missed the opportunity to be present on the Sheep Islands with a hotel, which indicates a golden future for tourism.

As one makes his bed, so he must party: hostels

Hostels enjoy higher status in the Nordic countries than they do at home. There they are also known as "guesthouses" and represent the cheapest option for overnight stays – aside from holiday homes. Their furnishings and features differ in terms of quality: usually they offer guests a few different rooms with shared use of a kitchen.
All guesthouses on the various islands are listed on the webpages of the tourist information offices.

In Tórshavn this is the most popular:
62°N GUESTHOUSE: It may be a little shabby but its central location in the town means you can roll from your room straight to the pub, a restaurant or a supermarket. Very cosy!

As one makes his bed, so he must fly: camping

Tents, camping, the romance of the caravan – for a long time, these were regarded by the Faroese as the practices of "pitiable" tourists. However, the Scandinavians would never dream of pointing their fingers and saying "I told you so" in a know-it-all manner when the first balmy summer breeze sent the idealist's tent flying, gluing it high up onto the 600-metre rock face. He is far more likely to say: "Come on, you can stay with me." But over the last few years, with the growth of the leisure-loving society, a trend has developed here too. Now the Faroese, with children and dogs in tow, sometimes go looking for a cosy spot themselves on warm (14°C) weekends, and they enjoy barbeques outside their camper vans, grilling as if there were no tomorrow.
What could be more natural than to rediscover the campsites that have since time immemorial been built only for form's sake? Today, in these mobile quarters you'll come across not only the caravans on their way to Iceland but also the new leisure time Vikings.

> After intensivly renovation, the campsite in Tórshavn is showing itself in best shape again.
> Tip: The campsites on Eysturoy in Æduvík and in Eiði have a great and unique location..

As one makes his bed, so he must live: holiday homes

Renting a holiday home is by far the most sensible option for a fishing holiday.
Information on a huge choice of houses that can sleep any number of people can be found on the webpages of the tourist information centres or via the relevant internet provider.
These houses, known on the Faroe Islands as "summerhouses", are usually the houses of the grandparents or parents of the landlord. They are not lived in because their owners have moved to live in Tórshavn to work.
Resourceful Faroese also rent out newly renovated beachfront homes and apartments.
The price for a whole house per night is often lower than that for a hotel room.

Finding the best of the best

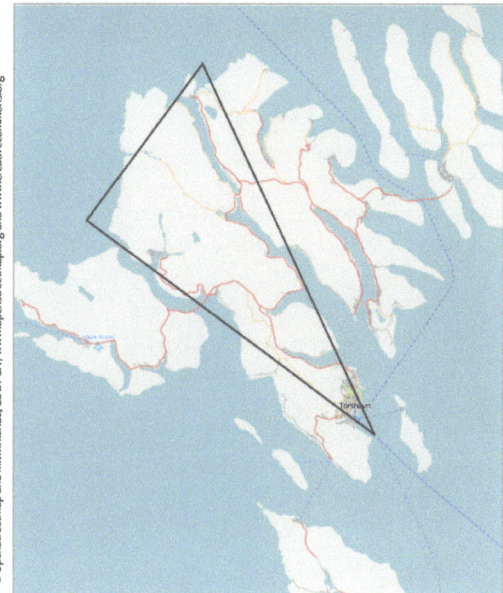

The island of Streymoy, where the capital Tórshavn is located, is also where the core business of fishing is done. From here you can decide spontaneously whether you want to head out to sea for angling or to fish for brown trout, sea trout or salmon, before going for a beer in Tórshavn when you return. Concentrate your search for a holiday home on the areas around the towns of Eiði, Hvalvik, Vestmanna, Kvívík, Leynar and Tórshavn itself.
Then you'll basically be at the centre of the action and can easily go on trips to Vagar, Sandoy or Eysturoy. You should also consider setting aside the time to spend a few days at the sea trout "Eldorado" on the most southerly island, Suđuroy.

Useful Information

When you board the ferry Norröna on your way home, you can put your haul of fish into a **freezer**; that way it will stay fresh for you until you arrive in Denmark.

Should you find yourself on the Faroe Islands around Midsummer, you should head to the **Stornfelli** mountain plateau on the night of the solstice. From there you have panoramic 360° views and can see how the sun really never sets.

To save on expensive roaming charges on your mobile, buy a **prepaid card**. On the Faroe Islands, Føroya Tele and two other smaller providers share the market. The whole archipelago has excellent internet coverage throughout the country.

When you buy goods that you intend to take home, ask the salesperson for a **Tax Free Form**. You'll be able to reclaim the VAT at the air- or seaport when you leave.

Chapter 3

The Strike of Thor´s Hammer

The Capital Tórshavn: "And though it be but little…"

Around half of the whole Faroese population lives in Tórshavn, which is one of the smallest capital cities in the world. Tórshavn is the centre of everything. You'll find a lively social scene here complete with restaurants, pubs, shops, pharmacies, a hospital and secondary schools. As Paris is to France, where all the motorway signs tell you how far you are from the capital, when you're on the Faroe Islands you can't avoid Tórshavn. And that is a good thing. Tórshavn is a wonderfully manageable town with a very small centre. Everything you're looking for is here. Two picturesque harbours flanked by cafés and restaurants give the town its maritime character. And just a few steps from the heart of the town you'll see family homes in open areas with gardens in which children bounce around on trampolines.

The first settlement and the location of the Løgting (Assembly of the Vikings) was, from 850 B.C., the rocky peninsula of Tinganes, upon which parts of the government administration are still housed.

When German lawyer and ornithologist Carl Julian Graba travelled to Tórshavn for the first time in 1838, he wrote:
"As we entered the harbour, our captain said: there stands your residence, but I was unable to see cultivated land, or houses, much less so a city, although I was within a rifle shot's reach. Only the pale green of the grass and the grey of the rocks were in sight, until the eye could more clearly make the distinction between objects, namely houses or rather huts that were of the same colour as the land, in that they consisted of wooden planks below and upon them roofs of grass. A little shudder took hold of me at the thought that this was said to be the grandest place on the Faroe Islands and that I would be here for several months."

Much has changed since this time, if not everything. And in some cases they have even turned back to some of the things of old…

Enjoy your dinner! But where?

Cafés, Bars and Restaurants in Tórshavn unfortunately are subject to regular changes in ownership, and – subsequently – in quality aspects. This is of minor importance however, since the most favourite and most strongly frequented are in the hands of only a few top dogs anyway.
Thus the Hotel Føroyar in Tórshavn not only manages the famous five star hotel but every fancy restaurant in town. But this is not a disadvantage. Quite the opposite: Those restaurants are a culinary revelation, focusing on the unbeatable freshness of the domestic sea food. These are the addresses that are worth visiting and an early booking is strongly advisable.

ÁARSTOVA, Gongin 1, Tórshavn, Tel 333 000
Picturesque location and ambitious kitchen with a large selection of domestic fish and lamb dishes.
BARBARA, Gongin 4-6, Tórshavn, Tel 331 010
Named after the most famous female figure in Faroese literature.
Small, secluded, hard to find, very cosy – serves only sea food.
RÆST, Gongin 8, Tórshavn, Tel 411 300
The building and menu couldn't be more authentic. Pure Faroe cuisine!
SKEIVA PAKKHÚS, 19 Sigmundargøta, Tórshavn, Tel 773 300
Perfect location right at the harbor and an excellent example of a smart implementation of a hipster restaurant in historical buildings.
THE TARV, Undir Bryggjubakka 3-5, Tóshavn, Tel 411 400
Like all the restaurants mentioned above, it belongs to the Hotel Føroyar chain and impresses with its interior design in a famous historical house at the harbor.
The best steakhouse on the Faroe Islands and the author's absolute favorite restaurant!
KATRINA CHRSITIANSEN, 6 Bringsnagøta, Tórshavn, Tel 313 243
This restaurant belonging to the Hotel Hafnia offers a good selection of local cuisine and it is worth a visit not only for the tasteful ambience.

Finger, Fast & Bar Food

For a quick bite to fill your belly after fishing, to lay the ground for an evening at the pub or, of course, as a cure for a hangover.

HVONN, Tórsgøta 11, Tórshavn
Brasserie on the first floor of the Hotel Tórshavn, very popular among the Faroese – good variety.
IRISH PUB, Grím Kambansgøta 13, Tórshavn
Above the seamen's pub Glitnir and furnished in the style of an Irish pub. Lovely view over the harbour. The pork chops are still beaten and breaded fresh by the chef every day.
PANAME CAFÉ, 4 Vaglið, Tórshavn
In the cozy building of the historic H.N. Jacobsen bookshop.
In the hands of a very ambitious owner who learned his culinary skills in Paris.
Very popular amongst the locals and the tourists.
BURGER KING, R. C. Effersøes Gøta 31, Tórshavn
In the SMS shopping centre.

There are, of course, many more imaginative chefs and smart gourmet facilities on the Faroe Islands – all of whom offer a level of quality and cleanliness that you can trust.

All through the night: from the quayside bar...

The islands don't have a long pub tradition. Drinking alcohol didn't used to be seemly, and certainly not in public. The first licenses were awarded only hesitantly to restaurants and cafés. But it is fun: when the ban on serving alcohol outdoors was lifted a few years ago, the first benches and tables appeared outside pubs the very next day.
Some tips for the thirsty – tried, tested and then tried again...

GLITNIR, Grim Kambans Gøta 13, Tórshavn
The author's favourite watering hole. Managed with a strict but loving hand by the proper Faroese Karli and Hans. It looks a little sober at first glance but beer haze and countless stories of fates at sea hang in the air.
IRISH PUB, directly above Glitnir.
Good bar food and Irish music til down at the weekend. Best craic in town!
ESSABARR, Áarvegur 7, Tórshavn
In the quaint setting of the old grocery store and hence very popular with tourists.
It used to be one of the top locations - today unfortunately a bit concept-less due to frequent changes of the tenants.
MIKKELLER, Gongin 2, Tórshavn
Branch of the Danish craft beer brewery. The bill will be expensive if you are thirsty for beer.
HVONN, Tórsgøta 11, Tórshavn
On the ground floor of the Hotel Tórshavn. Casual lounge atmosphere with cocktail bar character.
SIRKUS, Grím Kambansgøta 2, Tórshavn
Right next door to Hvonn but the exact opposite:
the twin pub of the very successful Sirkus in Iceland. More for the alternative crowd.
TÓRSHØLL, Sverrisgota 22, Tórshavn
Are you looking for an absolute insider tip, an original pub where no tourist or hipster is guaranteed to get lost? Then this is it.
BLÁBAR, Niels Finsensgøta 23, Jazz and Blues Bar. Only open on weekends. Very nice.

...to the beat lounges!

Depending on what exactly it is you're looking for – glamour, ambience or a few cheeky drinks – you'll find it in Tórshavn, as long as you observe a simple ground rule that could make great demands of your stamina.
No nocturnal goings-on begin before midnight and consequently they only finish at breakfast time. And why not? Nothing is certain, not even whether you'll get up in the morning.
If you don't party today you may not get another chance. That's why the Faroese make time for it because everything can be over so quickly. There is hardly any other nation that enjoys the pleasures of life in such a boisterous way.
Joviality rules the streets here without things ever turning nasty: they sing but they don't get aggressive.

Ah, those Fishing Stores!

Many Faroese buy their equipment when they're on holiday abroad. Internet orders are taxed at an astronomically high rate, making them advisable only in emergencies. People tie their own flies, and of course other rules apply for professional fishermen.
However, should you need something at short notice, here are three good places to head for:

JÓGVAN WEIHE, Stiðjagøta 10, Tel: 35 38 97
This shop specialises in outdoor clothing and equipment for professional and sport fishing. It has a large assortment of equipment for sea fishing. The needs of the fly fisherman are also catered for. Ask for Charles.
SVEND KROSSTEIN, Falkavegur 6, Tel: 34 46 00
This is actually a specialist plumbing store, but the family have been dedicated fly fishers for generations and have made room in a corner of their shop for a very reasonable range. With Hardy, and others.
VAGABOKHALD, Skaldavegur 1, 370 Miðvágur, on the Ilse of Vagar, Tel 232379
The heart of a true fly fisherman beats in the chest of Hjørleif Joensen and so since his retirement he is selling in a small shop in his house for very moderate prices such renowned companies like Simms, Scott and Arctic Silver. It is best to contact him before by phone.

You can buy bait from Jógvan Weihe: frozen shrimps and mackerel!

Shopping diversity. For the most part

There is hardly anything that you can't buy in Tórshavn.
It's only now and again that you'll find yourself standing in front of partially empty shelves. Everything has to be brought here by ship – one of the main reasons why prices are almost twice as high as they are in mainland Europe.

In the centre of Tórshavn, you'll find the more traditional shops that have been family-owned for generations. Modern shops are concentrated in the industrial area to the northwest of the town or in the SMS shopping centre.

There are numerous small shops over three floors in the SMS centre, and on the basement level you'll find the best grocery store on the Faroe Islands, along with a pharmacy.
Address: SMS, á Trapputrøðni, 100 Tórshavn

Grocery Shopping: from caviar to tinned sausage

In the **Miklagardur** supermarket (on the basement level of SMS, see page 46), no wishes are left unfulfilled.
There is no shop on the islands that offers so much choice and fresh produce.
There are, admittedly, two flies in the ointment.

The first has already been mentioned: the prices. Shopping should be done with care and with an eye on the price tags, otherwise you're in for a nasty surprise at the checkout. Or later when opening your credit card bill.

The second drawback is the paucity of regional products like fresh seafood.
Having said that, if you want to try Faroese classics such as lamb sausage, dried fish or "Skerpikjøt", you'll find them here, along with guacamole, Parma ham or some gorgonzola to top off the day's catch.

The other food stores on the island offer a rather more down-to-earth range of basic foods that will keep you going if you're reluctant to make your way to the capital.

Alcohol Consumption:
no longer drinking like the Vikings

There is a contradiction in the Nordic relationship with alcohol:
they're somehow able to drink and to disapprove of it at the same time.
Whether this can be traced back to a strong religious streak or to the desire to increase tax revenues is another question.

Alcohol could not be bought on the islands right up to the 1970s. If you paid the taxes and had the documentation to prove it, you were allowed to order a certain allowance from Denmark, which would then be delivered by ship. This was usually limited to six bottles of wine, the first of which would be empty soon after its arrival.

Things are different today, thank goodness, even though you still cannot buy beer at a petrol station or a supermarket. Apart from licensed cafés, pubs and restaurants, the only place you can buy alcoholic drinks is at one of the specialist spirits shops. There is one on each of the larger islands.

The one in Tórshavn is:
Rúsdrekkasøla Landsins at Hoyvíksvegur 67, Miðlon, Tel: 34 04 00

> There has recently opened a new brewery in Tórshavn with a modern, stylish concept:
> **OY Brewing**, 4 100 Falkavegur

The Nordic House: something for everyone!

Just as the Hotel Føroyar, integrated as it is into the landscape, towers above the rooftops of the capital to the southwest, so too the Norðurlandahúsið, which is an architecturally similar structure, watches over the residents to the northwest.
With its grass roof and squat design it is hardly noticeable from the outside.
The inside, however, offers generously sized halls for concerts, meetings and exhibitions.
Bill Clinton and Al Gore have both given speeches here.
Its cafe is also very popular for a quick lunch if you're not in the mood of looking for a parking space in the city center.

Address: Norðari Ringvegur or nlh.fo for the programme.

Weather-proof alternatives to dust catchers

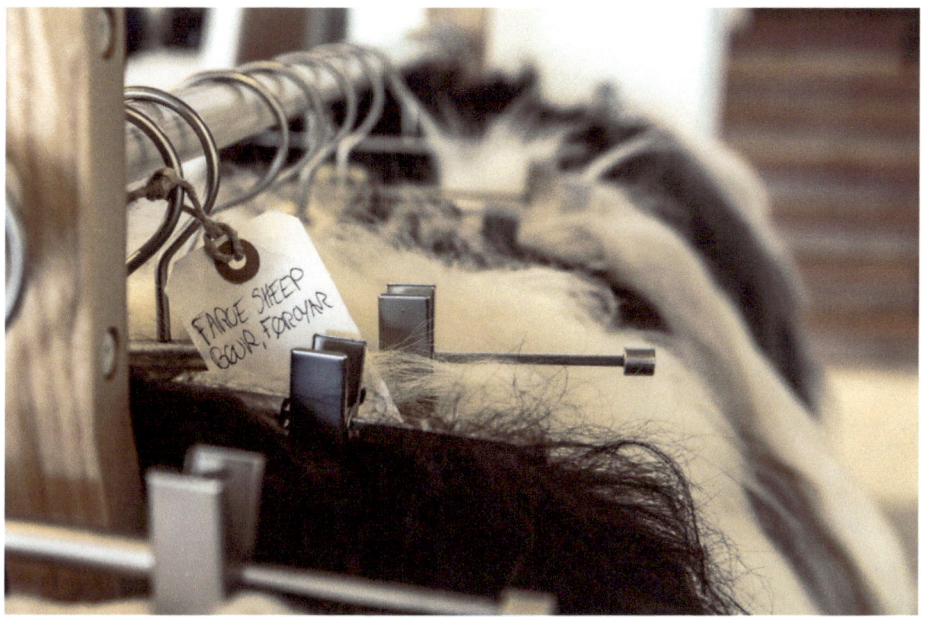

Souvenir buyers often head back home with a soft toy of a puffin or a key ring in the form of a seagull. Why not try something different?

The Faroe Islands are famous for their knitwear. You might argue that this is true of many Scandinavian countries, especially Norway, but beware! The famous Norwegian pullovers don't originate only from Norway at all, but rather from the Faroe Islands, Iceland and the Shetlands.

There are many good shops downtown.
The owners are charming, the buildings are inviting, and every fisherman is sure to find a woolly jumper or some angora underwear to keep them warm in force 9 winds and relentless rain. A very practical souvenir!

At the Harbour: lots of flair in a small space

When you look at a characteristic Faroese boat with its Viking-esque design, it's almost as if you can still feel the ghost of the thunder god Thor. You see them everywhere in the two picturesque marinas that are separated by the Tinganes peninsula and that form the beating heart of Tórshavn.

The eastern harbour is mainly used as a landing stage for the large ferries and cruise ships. It is the older part and is therefore lined with lovely old buildings. This is where the ships of the Hanse docked, which carried goods such as grain, wood and salt.
You can pay a visit to several cafés or have a meal in one of the restaurants, which are right on the harbour.

The western part of the harbour has a lovely little promenade and gives way to the docks at the furthest end.

In good weather, it is very tempting to linger on the benches and in the cafés.

Walks through the Past

Congratulations! If you can see this carved symbol on the ground before you, not only do you have eagle eyes, you are also standing on a thingstead, a site where the Vikings held their assemblies in days gone by. The symbols date back to the sixteenth and seventeenth centuries and are located on the headland of **Tinganes**, the oldest past of Tórshavn. The small, black houses, with their characteristic grass roofs and drying huts to store fish and meat, appear to be crouched down, packed closely together to protect themselves from the winds and the storms. The red buildings of the government administration are also located on Tinganes.

Directly next to the anchorage of the Norröna is the fort of **Skansin**. It too is a positively stereotypical example of the miniature world in which one finds oneself here, because as a "fort" it is anything but capital...
Nonetheless, it has served important purposes: in the eighteenth century it was tasked with protecting the Faroe Islands – using Danish canons that can still be seen today – from Saracen raids. In the Second World War it also served as a military base for the English, alongside their own canon. The fort's canons, however, have only ever been fired in salute.

Markets: cod not spuds

You won't find a vegetable or a farmers' market in Tórshavn as we know them back home – due to a lack of vegetables and farmers.

You do, however, sometimes come across fishermen offering their haul for sale at the harbour. Keep your eyes open for fulmars, cod, etc.

Highly recommended:
Carl August Arge. He regularly offers his catch right after hauling in at sea at the port of Vágsbotnur. You can see him standing there next to other fishermen.
Like many other Faroese, he also uses Facebook to inform his customers about his range and sales times.
Why not support them and add something extra to your dinner!

Useful Information

Today there are many websites and apps for the interested travelers. We particularly recommend the **"What's on"** page on visitfaroeislands.com. It informs you about all upcoming events.

You need a **parking disc** to park in the city centre (signposted). But you can park for 8 hours in the big car park by the second harbour without a parking disc.

There are **public toilets** between the Hotel Tórshavn and the Tórshavn Kommuna, as well as in the bus station.

The **bus station** for all routes around the Faroe Islands is next to the anchorage of the ferry Norröna.

The Faroe Islands are very tourist-friendly: there are large **rubbish bins** at almost all parking and sightseeing bays along the traffic routes. And everything is very clean.

It's actually quite unusual to give **tips** on the Faroe Islands, at least with small amounts. It is, however, appropriate to tip in restaurants when you've enjoyed service lasting some time.

If you need **medical attention** go directly to the hospital in Tórshavn:
Streymoy Landssjúkrahúsið, J. C. Svabos gøta 43, Tel: 30 45 00
Emergency number: 112

Chapter 4

„Who is Who" on the Faroe Islands

The Big Three on the Faroe Islands are salmon, brown trout and sea trout - with the cod and its conspecifics as worthy runners-up

First things first:
The freshwater fauna of the Faroe Islands is not as diverse as you might expect. There are no members of the carp family or species such as smelt, perch, pike or other non-predatory fish. The only natives here are the brown trout, the Arctic char in limited numbers, and the three-spined stickleback and the nine-spined stickleback in a few lakes.
In some waters that are connected to the sea one comes across eels as well as the salmon and the sea trout.
Because heavy rain falling on the riverbeds drains away so quickly, fishing activity is concentrated exclusively on the lakes. These lakes are of profound interest not just to fishermen but also represent an important object of study for biologists. Because Faroese waters are right on the boundary between the Arctic and Europe, you might expect a rich variety of different species and organisms. The opposite is actually the case. These waters are oligotrophic, meaning that they are habitats with low nutrient values and only a few life forms. In the isolation of the Atlantic, an ecosystem that is unique to these islands has developed and has survived almost without any external influence such as natural immigration, introduction or stocking. As a result, the Faroese inland waters are still "virginal", so to speak. Its species are genetically pristine and of a purity that is rarely encountered these days. Faroese lakes differ greatly in terms of food supply, size and fish density, as well as in terms of the size of the brown trout, which grow particularly slowly on the Faroe Islands. As a sign of trust in fishermen, one still has great freedom on the lakes and you don't need a license to fish, although every lake is privately owned.
Nature reveals its most beautiful aspect to you here – and this should be conserved. Respect the country; it's a privilege to be here. Don't press down any fences and above all else, observe the practice of catch and release if the lake appears to be a little "empty".

Why the horn of plenty is so full

What makes the sea around the Faroe Islands so rich in fish, and the fish so good to boot? It's quite simple: the islands lie at exactly the spot in the Northeast Atlantic where the warmth of the Gulf Stream meets the cold stream from the north. That's a recipe for rich fishing grounds. In addition, the sea temperature stays constantly low at between 6 to 12 degrees Celsius. Moreover, the fish grow very slowly and as a result have very firm flesh. For these reasons fish from Faroese waters are considered to be among the best in the world and are first choice for exquisite cuisine.

The fish species used commercially include the herring, spiny dogfish, the flounder, the black halibut, cod, mackerel, the rose fish, haddock, plaice, hake, pollack, sole, sprats and turbot, and less commonly the brown shrimp.

The main interest for fishermen when deep sea fishing is cod, coalfish, pollack, haddock, ling, catfish, redfish, mackerel and various types of flatfish.

And for the very brave among us, perhaps the porbeagle and halibut, which can comfortably grow to a size of two meters.

The V.I.F. (very important fish): Salmo salar

OK.
The Faroe Islands is not a classic salmon fishing location. There are no noble families with castles, salmon rivers or overpriced lodges next to ranging currents. Salmon fishing is done on lakes here.
In all fairness it should be mentioned that there are only two managed salmon lakes on the Faroe Islands and these are intensively fished at certain times. But salmon fishing is a very special passion and challenge here. Some Faroese buy holiday homes only 30 miles from where they live just so they can be that little bit closer to the action during the season, which lasts from August until mid-October.
The Faroese Sport Fishing Association has around 300 members and takes an active role in breeding and stocking. They have primarily taken the genetics of Icelandic salmon so as to establish these islands as a home for salmon.
This kind of passion in the country has produced brilliant fly fishermen, who can catch up to nine salmon a day. What sounds so easy is more of a challenge on the Faroe Islands than elsewhere: the fish can see extremely well in clear lakes. You have to let the fly hit the water far away from the line and take care when allowing it to submerge. Whoever is able to catch Salmo salar here is a master of his trade.
But if you're not a fly fisher you'll be relieved to hear that under certain circumstances more fish are caught with spinners or a shrimp on the hook. That is also allowed.

The Diva: sea trout, Salmo t.trutta

An excellent Faroese fisherman once said that he did not consider salmon fishing to be the supreme discipline, but rather fishing for sea trout. Anyone who has ever done battle with a salmon may well now be shaking their head in disbelief. Anyone who tries to catch a sea trout will, however, quickly concede that that man was right, despite the fact that they are in greater numbers everywhere – from the sea, via the lakes that are connected to the sea to the brackish water drainage channels. There are also moments when they just lap in the fjords like at home in a fish pond. But these beasts are devilishly hard to catch. They wilfully ignore all manner of flies and other means of persuasion with improbable shrewdness.
And even when you outwit them they fight to the last. A hat-tip to both the fish and the happy fisherman!
There are no regulations on the Faroe Islands with regard to fishing season. Sea trout is the true wealth of the country.
They feed predominantly on sand eels, small shellfish and amphipods, and as a result their flesh is a deep red. In winter months they move to freshwater areas to spawn and they prefer to stay in saltwater, especially in areas with sandy ground. Small to medium-sized fish are most common but you'll come across this species in various sizes in Faroese waters.

The Model: brown trout, Salmo trutta

The author's favourite fish – not just because of its beauty, which it parades as if self-evident, or its richness of colours in all conceivable nuances and forms. It's doubtful whether studies have been carried out on this topic, but even a layman can confidently postulate the theory that no brown trout is identical to any other, just as no whale fin is the same as any other. Their character and behaviour also range from easily accessible and communicative to complete and utter rejection.

The observant fisherman quickly comes to the realization that the brown trout, alongside the sea trout, represents the Faroe Island's true delicacy. It inhabits all the lakes here and appears in various hues and sizes. One fallacy should, however, be avoided: the bigger the lake, the bigger the fish. This is wrong, as the opposite is often the case. It is better to rely on another correlation: the more inaccessible the waters, the more numerous the fish. Therefore, here's a recommendation: take a tent and a sleeping bag and set off on a mountain hike on a warm June evening. Then your catch could break some records.

Having said that, on the Faroe Islands you should always keep in mind that – in contrast to the lakes of continental Europe, where food is abundant – Salmo trutta only grow very slowly in these nutrient-poor lochs. A fish of 30 to 40 centimetres is already as old as Methuselah, and has earned the right to be put back.

The lonely, fragile one:
char, Salvelinus alpinus faroensis

According to scientific findings, the so-called Arctic char, Salvelinus alpinus, is only to be found in four Faroese lakes.
Unfortunately, it is not worth going after these delicate fish. They are the very opposite of their cousins in Iceland or Greenland, being very small specimens.
With a maximum lifespan of five to nine years, they only grow to a size of around 20 cm. Competition for food against the brown trout in the nutrient-poor lakes is so great that there isn't much left for everyone.
It does, however, have the honour of being a separate species:
Salvelinus alpinus faroensis, species alpinus faroensis.

As a responsible angler, treat this fish with the necessary respect and release it again!

Fish with migration background

Since this book is set on completeness, the following pages will acquaint you with a couple of species that might at first puzzle you once you got them landed – because they neither belong to the classical fly fisher prey nor are indigenous to the Faroe Islands.

This picture for example shows a Pacific pink salmon (*Oncorhynchus Grobusch*), a female fish to be precise, caught by the author on the Faroe Islands. Its occurrence is quite out of the ordinary, because its natural habitat is the entire North Pacific Ocean, both along the American west coast and the Asian east coast. So how did this fish make its way into European waters? As off the 1950s, Russian scientists tried to domicile this species in the White Sea for the purpose of being an additional source of food – with mediocre success. Nevertheless, from there it gradually spread all along the Norwegian coast, primarily in water zones that correspond to the climatic conditions of their home waters. Today we even hear of exploding numbers in all European rivers, because this fish skillfully knows how to fill the void that the decline of the Atlantic salmon leaves. A pink salmon grows for two years in salt water and then migrates to the tributaries of the freshwater zones to spawn in summer.

After a three- to four-month hatching period, juvenile fish initially stay in the coastal area and later move into the open sea, always in a two-year cycle. This fish is basically not a direct competitor to the Atlantic salmon and sea trout, because it spawns much earlier and further downstream. Therefore, the young fish migrate into the sea earlier. All three species share the same feeding grounds for a only a short period in early summer. Furthermore we all know that the Pacific salmon in contrast to the Atlantic salmon dies immediately after spawning.

An American in his wedding suit

It can happen that one lands such a colorful fella, and then, scratching one's head, wonders what Faroese species this might be.
The answer is: none at all.
This is a rainbow trout or steelhead.
They are not indigenous to the Faroese waters, but were left behind by abandoned aquacultures, proving themselves to be great survivors. Today these fish enjoy their liberty mostly in harbor areas such as in Vestmanna and in summertime (June / July) start wooing willing brides in bright rainbow colors.

The Underdogs of the Saltwater: flatfish

When standing on a sandy beach doing a spot of sea fishing, you should take care not to tread on a flatfish.
Seriously, it is really unsettling to see how they flap about around your boot with their wave-like swimming movement.
Using a good fly or mackerel strips and shrimp for the hook you can switch to fishing off the breakwater in next to no time and start picking out the fish one after the other.
The most common coastal inhabitants are the flounder, the lemon sole, the common dab and the plaice.

Big fish – no effort

That fact that as a seaworthy angler you can go fishing in open waters and catch capital cods from a boat is anything but a secret on the Faroe Islands.
But this book was written by a fly fisherwoman primarily for fly fisher, therefore here is one tip you might not have heard of before:
It is also possible to catch very big cod with the fly and from the shore.
And to praise our craft even more it is a given that the fly is even more successful than natural bait, spinners, wobblers & co.
Just place yourself near the drains of one of the many fish factories, let a sinking line sink to the bottom and slowly strip it with an attractive fly slightly raised above the bottom.
With any luck you will be rewarded with a big bite!
One little drawback however: Please note that the area between the bottom and the surface is also home to hundreds of coal fish, so there you are most likely to hook one of them.

The Classics: cod, ling, pollack, etc.

Here are a few more kinds of fish that can be caught at **deep sea fishing** around the Faroe Islands, with the standard sizes given, as well as the size of the biggest specimen caught on fishing trips.

COD, standard 2–7 kg, biggest fish caught 13 kg
HADDOCK, standard 1.5–2 kg, biggest fish caught 3.4 kg
HALIBUT, standard 3–10 kg, biggest fish caught 80 kg
PLAICE, standard 1.5–2 kg, biggest fish caught 3.6 kg
CUSK, standard 1–3 kg, biggest fish caught 3.5 kg
FLOUNDER, standard 600–700 g, biggest fish caught 700 g
LING, standard 2–4 kg, biggest fish caught 7 kg
STRIPED CATFISH, standard 3–4 kg, biggest fish caught 6.8 kg
MACKEREL, standard 800–900 g, biggest fish caught 1.3 kg
WHITING, standard 1–1.5 kg, biggest fish caught 2.7 kg
POLLACK OR SAITHE, standard 3–4 kg, biggest fish caught 8 kg
PORBEAGLE, standard 100–130 kg, biggest fish caught 222 kg

Chapter 5

Tight lines!

There are no guarantees that you'll catch a lot of fish, but armed with these tips you'll increase your chances.

What makes the Faroe Islands different to other fishing regions are the extreme changes in conditions. There are many countries where they claim you can experience all the seasons in one day – but here it really is the case. And that is also true for the difference in weather between one island and another. You should therefore be equipped accordingly, both in terms of gear and clothing. The best approach is to be ready for ANYTHING, from a gentle breeze all the way up to wind force 9, from sun to fog to beating rain.

The one advantage, however, is that temperatures do not fluctuate all that much – they usually stay between 8 and 12° Celsius.
The most pleasant fishing conditions prevail with northerly winds in summer. Then the wind comes from behind you at many fishing spots and the wave crests are moderate.
Southerly winds usually bring stormy weather conditions and a lot of rain, the latter not always being a disadvantage when fishing!

When preparing for a fishing trip always consider the following aspects regarding your waters of choice – since they have to be in perfect balance if you wish to be successful:

Season. E.g. it makes no sense fishing for salmon in May.
Temperature. Try arousing Faroese trout at temperatures below 11°C, I dare you...
Wind. Direction or force. It's calm today? Then better go for brown trout.
Time of day. Sea trouts are much easier fooled in darkness.
Rain. Has there been any or recently enough rain? Because that what it takes to wake up salmon and sea trouts.
Tides. Disbelievers may well try fishing for sea trout during high and low tide – just to notice that the best time is right before high tide reaches its peak.
Lunar phases. Some people – and not just Esoteric – swear by it: full moon and particularly high tide is the secret to success.

Still waters run deep: where to fish

RIVERS: Let's address this downer at the outset: rivers are practically irrelevant when it comes to fishing on the Faroe Islands. Sadly. Because of the geological configuration of the islands, the rivers are just drainage channels for accumulating rainfall.
MOUNTAIN LAKES: These treasures of nature can be found on all of the Faroe Islands. And they sometimes contain treasures of their own, such as brown trout 75 cm long and weighing 4.1 kg, like the one caught by a Faroese fisherman using mackerel strip bait on a mountain lake of around 800 m2.
LARGER LAKES: There is one large lake on each of the islands of Vágar, Eysturoy and Sandoy. Ideal playgrounds for active fishermen.
BAYS: Here it's simply a case of looking at a map or following the directions given in this book! You'll catch sea trout, single salmon and flatfish in all bays that have freshwater inflows and sandy ground.
PIER: A hot tip: find a quay with an attached fish factory – there is a great number of them – and you'll soon be filling your bowl with saithe and cod.
SEA: You'll find plenty of advice on sea fishing in this book. See for example in chapter 11.

> No part of the Faroe Islands is further than around three miles from the sea and it's amazing how close together freshwater and saltwater fish can be found. Fishermen are spoilt for choice here. Chapters 6 to 10 contain a detailed list of the locations of the various bodies of water.

Endless Summer: the time to travel

This is where the hearts of fishermen start beating faster…

This picture was taken at midsummer. Before us is the view towards the sea, and only 10 metres behind the photographer is a freshwater lake to die for. Trout are smacking their lips and slurping in insects from the surface. The really big ones come up from the depths and almost jump onto land to take their catch.

This is all happening in June, when the sun never sets. You can practically fish for brown or sea trout 24 hours a day. In addition, calmer conditions prevail on sea, so you can fish for cod and others.

Alternatively, wait until the end of July/mid-August – that's when the salmon run begins. It's pointless to go after the Salmo salar before this time. There are no „Springfish" here. But because the salmon only succeed in their ascent if there is enough water flowing in the feeder channels, there has to be enough rainfall from the end of July.
The season ends in October (enquire after the exact dates because they vary). In any case, arriving here late in the season is not recommended. By then most fish are already very dark and the weather becomes increasingly rough.
The best time is considered to be the last weeks of August and the first weeks of September.

The formalities of a passion

Bureaucracy can be temperamental. The current regulations regarding licenses, prices and fishing regulations vary from time to time. You can read them again on the fishing cards, on the website of the Faroese fishing club (laks.fo) or compare them in conversation with local anglers.

Disinfection is not required. However, you should still act responsibly if you have previously fished in questionable waters.

You only need **licenses** for salmon fishing in Lake **Leynavatn** with its two small "companion lakes" **Mjáuvøtn** and for **Saksunarvatn**.
Day tickets can be purchased at various locations (you can find them on laks.fo).
Fishing cards and prices are always updated after the annual meeting of the
Føroya Sílaveiðufelag association in March each year.
Fishing regulations for the salmon lakes: Fishing prohibited on Sundays (special regulations in Saksun) / boats not allowed / no vehicles allowed on the shore / everyone under 18 years of age fishes freely / no regulations regarding the amount of taken fish. There is a size limit of 30 cm for all fish.
Fishing licenses or permits are not required on other freshwater lakes or at the sea. This generous behavior deserves appropriate respect and behaviour. It's best to ask the landowner for permission beforehand.

In **Leynar**, fishing is not allowed by Faroese law from **June 15th to September 30th** in the riverbed, on the beach and in the entire bay up to the lighthouse due to the salmon arriving. For the same reason, from **September 1st** it is not permitted to fish in any other **river** (if it has water) or riverbed connected to the sea. With the exception of the tidal areas.

There is an allowance of **exporting** 25 kilograms of fish. But only for private use!

Two words: Catch & Release

You'll very rarely come across Catch & Release when fishing on the salmon lakes of Leynavatn and Saksunarvatn, as it would make little sense. There are barely any **salmon** that do not come from the breeding programme of the Association and very few populations that derive from natural reproduction on the islands, so there is no need for you to feel bad when you take your fish away with you. The only reasons to release a fish in accordance with the conservation drill include really not having a use for the fish, or that the fish has already been in the fresh water for a long while and has become dark and emaciated.

It is a different case with **brown trout** in fresh waters. In the smaller lakes you should not land fish after fish because there is no fish stocking here. The whole population is natural stock that would certainly be decimated by incorrect fishing behaviour.

It's hard to say what state the **sea trout** is in because there have been no studies. One fact that is certain is that other animals such as the puffin, which feeds predominantly on the sand eel just like the sea trout, have dramatically diminished in numbers due to its decline. In addition, the increasing number of salmon farms with its fish lice is a huge problem for them!

Listen to your inner guidance on this. If you'd like to take a lot of fish home with you, charter one of the Faroese skippers, with whom you'll catch many kilo of high-quality fish, and all with a clear conscience.

What our food eats

This **sea trout** (see top picture) comes from the beach of Sandsvágur on the island of Sandoy, and it appears to have enjoyed more than a few sand eel. It also feeds on other small fish, amphipods, small crustaceans, mysid shrimp and worms.
It would have done better to avoid dessert, a small "Teal Blue & Silver" fly.

Smaller **brown trout** rely only partially on small fish as a source of food.
Most prefer benthic organisms – invertebrates that live on the water bed. Non-biting midge larvae and pupae (*Chironomidae* and related subfamilies such as the *Tanypodinae* and *Orthocladiinae*) are the main food for Faroese Salmonids. Water fleas (*Cladocera*) are another important source of food, mainly the *Eurycercus lamellatus*.

The pictures in the lower row show the typical inhabitants of Faroese lakes, both above and below the water. It is known that in some lakes the fish sometimes change their feeding habits, switching from benthic foods to small fish. This leads to a remarkable acceleration in growth rates and a longer lifespan.

There is such a thing as bad weather – and completely inappropriate clothing

Everyone has their own ideas and experience of what constitutes bad weather.

The gentleman in this picture is by no means a novice when it comes to fishing – he is actually the most experienced of all German holidaymakers to the Faroe Islands. And he is a legend.

But this chapter is not meant to force a dress code upon you if you feel that you are the best judge of your own resistance to the weather. This chapter is aimed at those readers who are still unsure as to how to arm themselves against rough conditions.

Quilted overalls have proved to be the most suitable attire for sea fishing trips.
When fishing for salmon and sea trout you'll need the whole range, depending on the weather, from waders (you're standing in the water for the most part) to multilayered outerwear. Modern Gore-Tex jackets are the first choice in this regard.

If it's brown trout you're after, your clothes should also be comfortable because you'll be covering some distance, and you might even have to climb a mountain or two. Some Faroese pack their things in a rucksack and get changed when they reach the lake.

For the flyfisher: rods, lines, leaders

For salmon fishing:
Rods and reels: weight category 7 to 9, rod length from 9 to 11 feet, only single-handed fly rods are used to fish. Very seldom switch or double handed rods.
Lines: Usually WF, floating lines are used, less often shooting heads.
Leaders/tippets: as an experienced fisherman you could even go for 23 mm

For sea trout fishing:
Rods and reels: as for salmon fishing, but going above weight category 7 is not recommended.
Lines: likewise usually WF, floating
Leaders/tippets: from around 21 mm

For brown trout fishing:
Rods and reels: long rods are the most suitable from 9 feet upwards, weight category 6, but a long rod in weight category 5 can also certainly be used.
Lines: WF, floating
Leaders/tippets: from 15 mm, usually 17 mm

The Big Question

Science is divided on this question. Friendships and marriages have been torn apart because of it. Fishing greats have been born and have fallen again, and yet there is hardly anything that is of more marginal importance than **the choice of fly**.
60% of the chance of a fish taking the bait is down to the fish itself. 30% is down to ability and 10% – admittedly – is the choice of fly. Fishermen usually take the fly with which they have caught before, and it will likely be the right choice of fly for them again.
Nevertheless, here are a few recommendations:

For salmon fishing:
Teal Blue & Silver, Hairy Mary, Red Francis, Shrimp Flies, and small tube flies, sizes 8 to 10

For sea trout fishing:
Teal Blue & Silver, March Brown, amphipod imitations like Flash Bach Adams, sand eel and shrimp imitations, around size 10

For brown trout fishing:
Bibio, Peter Ross, Woolly Bugger and dry flies, sizes 10 to 14

Tips for fishermen

- How are the clouds distributed? It would be grossly negligent to find yourself suddenly enveloped in fog during a trip to the mountains.

- Do as the Romans do: as a fly fisher, use a double rod length for the leader. That significantly increases your chances!

- Have a chat with the Faroese while you're fishing. They are very hospitable and will give you a wealth of good, well-intentioned advice.

- Use dark flies (like Hairy Mary) on dark days and light flies (like Teal Blue & Silver) on sunny days.

- And here is a very personal piece of advice: Don't lose too much time fishing at "inactive" waters. Look out for signs of life on the surface and cast directly towards the fish. It will surely take the bait. But if there are neither rings nor jumping fish – move on! On the Faroe Islands, the next water is just minutes away. Remember: Success depends on spotting the fish!

A very good website for the precise weather forecasts: yr.no

Chapter 6

Fishing on Streymoy, the Isle of Many Faces

Prepare to be amazed!

Streymoy is without doubt the most impressive of the Faroe Islands.
With a land area of around 144 square miles, the main island is not only the biggest, it is also where you'll find the most action.
This is where the capital city of Tórshavn is located.
This is where the two cultivated salmon lakes Leynarvatn and Saksunarvatn are.
And this is where you'll find the most options for your fishing holiday.

However, as a result, more fishermen come here and they all have to share the waters.
The map of Streymoy included in this book shows recommended spots that, experience tells us, promise fishing success.
Of course, you can go fishing with some success all around the Faroe Islands, but the places mentioned here are among the special hot spots.
Not included on the map are the numerous options for fishing at the sea shore and on the small mountain lakes. The latter in particular require a spirit of adventure, stamina and climbing ability and are therefore down to how brave you're feeling.
In addition, these mountain lakes are all privately owned and should not be fished without the permission of the landowner.

But even those who want to stick to the hot spots will have their hands full...

Don't miss: Tjørnuvik

Aesthetics for fishermen and lovers of nature and culture:
the journey to Tjørnuvik is worth it not only because of the sea trout that splash about in the waters on its fine sandy beach; it is also a must because of the spectacular location and the views towards the two famous rocks **Risin og Kellingin** (The Giant and the Witch).
Tjørnuvik is one of the six places on the Faroe Islands that should not be missed.
You will also pass by the largest waterfall on the Faroe Islands, the **Fóssa**, on the breathtaking drive to get there.
Tjørnuvik was one of the first Viking settlements, which is fully understandable considering this unique location.
Tip: don't neglect to explore the left-hand end with the view towards the sea. You'll find dramatically coloured caves opening out on an awesome vista. And if you're lucky, the odd saithe in the water.

You should definitely visit these places on the Faroe Islands:
On Streymoy: Tjørnuvik, Saksun, Kirkjubøur and Kvívík. Gjógv on Eysturoy, Viðareiði on Viðoy, Gásadalur on Vagar and Famjin on Suðuroy

The three best bodies of water around the legendary Saksun: 1. The Mighty Fjord

Just the drive from Hvalvik to Saksun is a very special experience that will make an impression on all who come here, not just fishermen. After a stretch of just over six miles through a secluded yet magnificent valley, the landscape opens out onto the romantically situated Saksunarvatn. Scattered around are a few holiday homes belonging to those fishermen lucky enough to have received permission to build a refuge here in the 1960s. The important spot is not hard to get to: keep left, drive straight on and park at the closed-off zone. Follow the tarmac path that leads you down to the basin of the fjord, where you'll find the so-called Pollur, a saltwater lake where water always flows. You can also walk further out to the sea. But, as ever, caution is advised. It is vital to be aware of the tide because flippancy or a lack of knowledge in this regard can be a matter of life and death on the Faroe Islands. It is thanks to a huge flood in the past that a sandy path leads out to the west today, although it is only traversable at low tide. The landscape was previously made up purely of rocks – now it is a breathtakingly beautiful sandy beach that also offers a great possibility of catching sea trout.

> Unfortunately - and as an obvious expression of the changing society due to the massive onset of tourism, there is now a turnstile in the middle of the valley where you have to pay for your entrance with a credit card.

2. The Ever-Exciting Pollur

Between the sea and the salmon lake of Saksunarvatn lies Pollur, a kind of intermediate station for all the fish that call this their home.
By nature it is a saltwater lake and as a result the tides are moving in and out.

Pollur is crystal clear. Its water is supplied by some of the large waterfalls in the area and, of course, by flow from the Saksunarvatn.
Because of this you could fish here for sea trout all year round, and you could even hook a Salmo salar in the period when the salmon gather for the run.
The subjunctive "could" is chosen deliberately; because just like the turnstile on its bank, the landowner of the Pollur has also **completely closed the water** to all anglers with the increasing stream of visitors. *(The only exception to fish there is for local residents, like the gentleman in the picture).*

3. Saksunarvatn, the Romantically Situated Salmon Lake

Saksunarvatn inspires joy in every fisherman's heart.
It is the house and home lake of the Faroese fly fishing celebrities, the Carlson brothers, who can often be seen leaving after a successful day with a few caught salmon under their arms.
What makes Saksunarvatn so pleasant is its manageability.
It can be very busy here some days but the lake can be fished almost from all sides.
As a rule, whole schools of fish make rounds along the lake's shoreline.
Less experienced fishermen can position themselves according to others to check out how their chances stand and where best casting position is.
The best of the Faroese fishermen cast selectively at groups of fish passing by.
With a bit of luck a salmon veers away from the group and takes the fly.
May it soon be one of yours!

You'll need a fishing licence. See page 73

Nesvík: Where the North Atlantic shrinks to a width of 220 metres

Narrow? Yes.
Peaceful? By no means.
In the straits below the bridge linking the islands of Streymoy and Eysturoy, and the towns of Nesvík and Norðskáli, preside the concentrated powers of the North Atlantic and its elemental tides, which any sensible person would do well to keep at rod's length. Even ships occasionally get stuck. But the abundance of fish here is unique.
And that's not all: the potential for new anecdotes is also without a match. Don't be surprised if your fish, once hooked, proceeds to orchestrate a sudden "escape", taking your whole line in the process. It's quite probable that a seal will be grinning at you a few minutes later, proudly showing you that he won the battle for the fish.

Fishing in Rivers: A General Note

This picture – taken at the same spot – shows a typical Faroese "river".

It shows clearly that the riverbeds on the Faroe Islands are, topographically speaking, only there to channel the downpours to the sea in the most direct way and usually at very steep gradients. They are shallow and rocky and are actually not fishable.

The only stretches resembling rivers, such as at Hvalvik for example (see next page), are just backwater areas of salt water.

All river areas are closed to any kind of fishing from 1 September until 1 May.
With exception of the tidal aereas.
All affluents to the **Leynavatn** are closed all year round as potential spawning waters.

The Stora at Hvalvik

Stora is the Faroese word for "river" and is therefore often to be seen on maps.
The stora between Hvalvik and Streymnes occupies an exceptional place, however, as it comes closest to our idea of a gently flowing river.
It has a relatively wide basin by Faroese standards, and shortly before the mouth of the river it spreads out into a small side delta. It is supplied by seawater and by the inflow of the river, which collects rainfall in Saksunardalur – the valley after Saksun – and flows into the sea here. This is a popular spot for friends of sea trout fishing all year round. At high tides, the Salmo trutta trutta like to come all the way up here to the large bridge that links the two villages.
At the end of July each year, the natural salmon population begins its run upriver. With any luck you'll catch yourself a good specimen.
Having said that, for any true fisherman, it is admiration for the animal that stands in the foreground, an animal that – driven by instinct – powerfully surmounts the challenges of dry, stony stretches far up into the valley direction Saksun to reach its spawning grounds. All the more macabre then the drama when they are pulled out of the few shallow pools. Fortunately there is an obligatory period of protection from 1 September.

 You can catch here: sea trout, salmon, mullet, eel and different kind of sea fish

Lakes that do not keep their promise

A look at the map of Vestmanna reveals five scenic mountain lakes which almost beg to try them out, particularly because they are well accessible by car. The road maybe tricky sometimes, but it makes up for it with breathtaking panoramic views.

All of those lakes underwent various changes in the past:
For example, some were well maintained "Put & Take" lakes and others even closed waters due to parasite infections.
These lakes sometimes also host large populations of brown trout and Faroese char in well-fed condition.

And here comes another „but": During the last years the electricity supplier SEV, which runs the hydroelectric power stations at the harbor, has drained a couple of lakes due to repair works (see picture above). After being reflooded, the lakes look as tempting as ever, yet they do not contain a single fish.

It is advisable to enquire about current regulations and fishing possibilities at the Tourist Office in Vestmanna.

Fishing in the Harbour: Where the fish go

The harbour of Vestmanna is quite a lively place. With its charming atmosphere and its status as an important hub, you are certain to get to know the place from various angles.
Those looking for information will find a well-run tourist office and those in the mood for adventure can get on board of one of the boats that go to the truly exciting boat trips to the bird cliffs.

But let's get back on topic: aquatic beasts.
Vestmanna has a lot to offer in this regard, even if the fish can be very tricky. There are two large hydroelectric power plants in the harbour area and all the sea trout and salmon passing by feel magically drawn towards the oxygen- rich water. As a result the waters around the power plants are also abundant places for the wily fisherman.

The energetic anglers among us can expect a really big show while fishing at the pier of the fish factory (Heyganesgota 3). Swarms of cod and coalfish cavort around the richly laid table for the disposal of leftovers in front of the drains (see also page 66).
Better not to fish on the weekends; because then the Eastern European workers march up to enjoy their fishing leisure time.

The Beach at Leynar:
the starting line for the large salmonides

Down at the beach of Leynar, is not only one of the most scenic landscapes of the islands, but also one of the most exciting areas for fans of Faroese sport fishing.

It is one of the best spots for sea trout and also where salmon and sea trout begin their ascent to the higher lakes Leynavatn and the upper and lower Mjáuvøtn.

However, it is essential to observe the restriction of fishing because of the salmon ascent from **June 15 to September 30** in the entire location:
It is then no longer allowed to fish in the river bed, on the beach and in the whole bay up to the lighthouse.

Over the Fish Ladder in Leynar

Here's a suggestion if you're looking for an encounter with the fish above water:

pack your lunch and a camera, set off to Leynar and watch the salmon and the sea trout on their run.

With much dedication and hard work, the Faroese Sport Fishing Association has built a fish ladder to make the climb to the lakes 100 metres above easier for the fish.

A fish counter has also been installed and a number of resting pools built, from which the Association takes parent animals for the breeding farms in Tórshavn every year.

Such an afternoon can also give a fisherman much joy and relaxation – even if it is just a short encounter outside the confines of the hunt.

Up the Leynavatn

Leynavatn can well be described as the main hot spot for salmon, and because it is located practically at the gates of Tórshavn this is also where most fishermen gather.
Those who like conviviality, who who enjoy having a chat with locals about the salmon or who could do with a few tips are in good hands there.
Leynavatn is without doubt the long-cherished favourite of the Faroese Sport Fishing Association. You'll come across up to 30 fishermen each day in the high season from mid-August until the end of September.
Fishing with flies is the norm, spin fishing is much less common, while those tenaciously fishing with glowing red floaters and shrimps are a rarity.
You can certainly leave these colleagues to their luck with a bit of a wink.

If you like your fishing a bit quieter then it is recommended that you get to the lake at dawn. The atmosphere is often spellbinding with gradually clearing wafts of mist, and the salmon are also less shy and more receptive at this time.

You'll need a fishing licence here. See page 73

The Two Lakes of Mjáuvøtn

Here's another tip for those who like it a bit quieter.
You'll rarely see a single fisherman standing on the shores of either of the two small lakes of Mjáuvøtn – such is the draw of the huge Leynavatn. One small drawback though is the through traffic behind you.

You shouldn't underestimate what these small bodies of water contain. Big fish can often be seen moving up the small stream of Leynavatn to the Mjáuvøtn, and the Sport Fishing Association also releases smolts here. This is a spot where many fishermen have even caught their first salmon.

> The fishing licence for Leynavatn also allows you to fish in these two lakes. See page 73

After Sea Trout in the Bays: 1. Kollafjørður

Admittedly, with its alternative harbour for Tórshavn and the fish processing plants, this spot doesn't exactly look like an inviting place to fish.
However, the small freshwater stream Dala, which enters the Kollafjoður at the end of the bay, must be very popular among sea trout because you can encounter them here all year round.
Or it might actually be the spices from the fish factory upstream that draw in the water-dwellers. In any case, one often drives past this spot and a fishing stop is worth it every time.

Kollafjørður is also an interesting fishing spot for friends of pier fishing.
There are several fish processing plants down by the sea at the quays. The catch from the trawlers and boats of the aqua cultures daily arrives and is processed immediately.
The fish residues are chopped up and pumped out of large pipes into the sea, where everything that has fins is already waiting.
Then it's just like in the popular German fishing documentary series:
„Rute raus, der Spaß beginnt!" (Rod out, the fun begins)
See the tips on pages 66 and 94.

2. Kalbaksbotnur, right next door.

On a good day, fishing in this bay is like fishing in a trout pond – fish as far as the eye can see.

Fishermen from Tórshavn would still have travelled by boat to Kalbaksbotnur up to the 1950s. In those days there was still no road suitable for cars leading there.
Then, during the Cold War, NATO built a listening post on the 700-metre peak above the bay, along with a road leading to the station below, the Oyggjarvegur.
This was still 300 metres above sea level, so you had to descend the mountain to go fishing and then climb up again.
 Since the beginning of the 1990s there has been a link road down below in the valley, which drove the sea trout away to begin with.

By now it appears that they have returned and you really have it easy if you decide to go after them.

Argir, the "Beat" of the Capital

Opposite the city hospital, between Tórshavn and Argir, lies a very beautiful beach with an inlet that flows over cliffs and under old bridges and out to sea.

It is a popular place for fishing enthusiasts from the capital who can go after sea trout practically on their doorstep.
What's more, the bay is full of history since the capital's Grindadráp is also held here.

 You can catch here: sea trout, salmon, and different kind of sea fish

Sightseeing Tips

This table can be seen in the Roykstova of the old farmhouse and museum in **Kirkjubøur**. Official guests of state are occasionally invited to partake of a feast around it. In doing so they are sitting around the wooden hatchway of a British steamship that sank off the Faroe Islands in 1895. The only survivor of the wreck was a sailor from Rostock by the name of Heinrich Anders. He had been floating in the water holding on to the hatchway for 14 hours before being washed up on the coast of Kirkjubøur.

In **Áir**, between Hósvik and Hvalvik, you can see a number of houses that are all painted in the same colour. This was the whale processing station of the Faroe Islands right up to the 1980s. There are still large whale bones, cauldrons, winches and landing ramps to be seen there.

Kvívík was one of the first Viking settlements and the ground layout of two longhouses can still be seen today. Children's toys were found during excavation work there, as well as a woman's shoe. A very similar shoe was also discovered in Paris.

The **Saksun** settlement with its lovely museum of local history and idyllic church is considered by travel journalists to be one of the most beautiful places in the world!

Chapter 7

Fishing on Eysturoy, the Majestic Isle

Mysterious and formidable – just like the waters!

A formidable island with more than 60 mountain peaks, among them the highest of the Faroe Islands, the Slættaratindur at 882 metres – this is Eysturoy.

You can fish in the bays here on your own initiative or, when conditions are good and after careful planning, set off to the small gems that are the mountain lakes.

Eysturoy will reveal the possibility of catching impressively sized brown trout. Don't be surprised if you catch one 75 centimetres in length and weighing eight pounds in mountain lakes that are just a pinhead on the map.

The Eiðisvatn

The dammed lake called Eiðisvatn came into being in the 1980s in the place of a small, magically located loch.
It is shaped today by two dams and is of such massive dimensions that it takes some time to circle it. But the Eiðisvatn is home to the largest brown trout on the islands and catching fish around 40 centimetres in length is the norm.
Unfortunately, taking boats out on the lake is not permitted, having been forbidden after a tragic accident.
The lake can, however, be fished from any point along the shore. The best spots are on the eastern shore where the streams and waterfalls flow in.

As with all lakes on the Faroe Islands, it is hardly worth going after trout when temperatures fall below 11° Celsius. The fish are not particularly active then, preferring to stay in deeper areas.

> It's easy to miss the approach to Eiðisvatn. Turn off to the right between the villages of Ljósá and Eiði, drive up the hill and keep to the right of the first dam wall.

The Two Contrasts in Eiði

Are you in the mood for sea trout? Or would you prefer to fish for brown trout? Preferably both at once?
Then give it a try in a beautiful bay in the village of Eiði. It is located in the northeast of the village and you can see the fishing spot from above when driving down.
The special thing about this place, however, is how it stands as a symbol of the proximity of two different worlds: salt water and fresh water (see picture on page 34). While the village lake, which serves as a local recreation area for families from Eiði and as a habitat for resting birds and swans, contains classic freshwater vegetation and a good stock of trout, the North Atlantic roars at the coastline with all its might barely 30 metres away. Big sea trout in it, but they are mostly to far out to reach. There is a narrow passage from the sea to the lake, which is used by small to medium-sized sea trout. They switch from one water to the other depending on their mood. Many anglers then mistake their caught sea trout for brown trout. Note that brown trout have red dots on their skin!
A few years ago the former soccer field by the village lake was converted into a campsite. Due to its particularly beautiful and romantic location, it is very popular with both the leisure Vikings and tourists. It is understandable that most of them keep their fishing rod in the water as part of the holiday program or paddle in high spirits with rubber dinghies on the lake, which unfortunately leads to a high fishing pressure and also affects the biotope enormously.

Sea Trout Bay at Skálabotnur

The Bay of Skálafjorður, close to the village of Skálabotnur, is captivating thanks to its perfect beach.
And that is something the sea trout also know to value. A fresh stream that channels much of the rainfall from the surrounding mountains into the sound is the icing on the cake, making conditions ideal.

What's more, if you park at Skipanesvegur (Route 10), at the confluence into Skalafjordur, you'll have a clear sight of the important points from above and will be able to estimate the numbers of fish sojourning in different areas.

 You can catch here: sea trout, salmon (Atlantic Salmon and Pink Salmon), also different kind of flat- and sea fish.

The Lake shrouded in Mystery

At the southern end of the island of Eysturoy, not far from Runavik, lies the lake of Toftavatn. It stands only 15 metres above sea level, has a depth of around 22 metres, and is often neglected by anglers as a destination.
It is the fourth largest lake on the Faroe Islands and the exceptional fauna that is to be found here, along with the wealth of legends that are in the air, make it a truly impressive place.
It is flanked by vast fields of heather and is said to be where trolls and elves get up to mischief.

It is one of only a few bodies of water in which sticklebacks and eels can be found.
There are plenty of brown trout, they feed mostly on zooplankton here, they stay small in growth and reach an average age of four years.
And the moral of the story: it's not always size that counts. Especially when magical beings have a hand in it.

Tip: when fishing, concentrate on the northeast side around the pedestrian bridges and the little transformer house.

"Listen to the sound of the river and you will get a trout." Irish proverb

On the entire archipelago and not just on Eysturoy, it is always worthwhile to pay attention to the coastal strips. Fish is everywhere.
But particularly interesting areas are small beaches and bays into which a freshwater inlet flows.
If the hotspots described in this book are already occupied by other anglers or if you just prefer to fish like an individualist on your-own, try one of these beaches:

- the bay in **Elduvík**: a wonderfully situated small village in the middle of nowhere
- the end of the bay in **Funningsfjørður**: sometimes with a real chance of salmon
- in **Oyndarfjørður**: the fresh water creeks at the church
- the beach at **Gøtugjógv**: here you can wade far out for a get together with the sea trout
- right next to it - the little river and beach in **Norðragøta**: here, too, you have to wait for the right moment when there is a lot of rainfall

Sightseeing Tips

The memorial in **Eiði** is very moving, with plaques commemorating the names and ages of those who lost their lives at sea.

There is a natural harbour in **Gjógv** that is used by fishermen because of its sheltered location in a ravine. The village as a whole is charming and is also appealing due to the abundance of sea trout in the bay.

You can watch the ships of the fish industry unloading at the harbour in **Runavik**.

At the most southerly point of Eysturoy, close to **Æðuvik**, is the old assembly place at Tinghella. It is visible from above but can only be reached by water.

You can drive via Leirvik on Eysturoy through an undersea tunnel to reach the second-largest town on the Faroe Islands, **Klaksvik**, on the island of Borðoy – which is only of limited interest. Klaksvik lives from fishing and highlights this with a huge monument in the form of a **fishing hook** on the approach to the town.

In contrast, the drive to **Viðareiði** on the island of Viðoy is worth it by all means. A spectacular panorama awaits you there. The wooden church with its adjoining vicarage is also interesting.

More and more popular among globetrotters is also a trip to the island of **Kalsoy**.
The **Kallur** lighthouse and the statue of the **Kópakonan** (seal woman) are one of the most breathtaking scenic impressions the Isles have to offer.
Even the James Bond film crew knew how to use this for the final blockbuster.

An insider tip: take the "Ritan" passenger ferry from Havannasund across the Fugloyarfjørður to the islands of **Fugloy and Svínoy.**

Chapter 8

Fishing on Sandoy, the Sweet and Gentle Isle

The weather's like Ibiza – but here it's the fishermen who party!

Admittedly that might be a bit of an exaggeration, but the weather on Sandoy does always seem to be a tad better than on the other islands.
This is probably down to the fact that Sandoy is, on the whole, somewhat flatter and stretches out towards the south. Here you can see large areas where hay or potatoes are grown.

The island is dominated at its centre by the relatively shallow lake of Sandsvatn, which is one of only a few lakes on the Faroe Islands that does not flow into the sea as a waterfall but rather has its own direct connection. The people of Sandoy are extremely friendly and open.
You often see families having picnics on the beach and children playing in the water.
As a fisherman, stomping towards the sea through the family idyll wearing the obligatory waders, Gore-Tex jacket and balaclava, you often feel like an astronaut on a different planet. It's quite likely that the locals think the same!

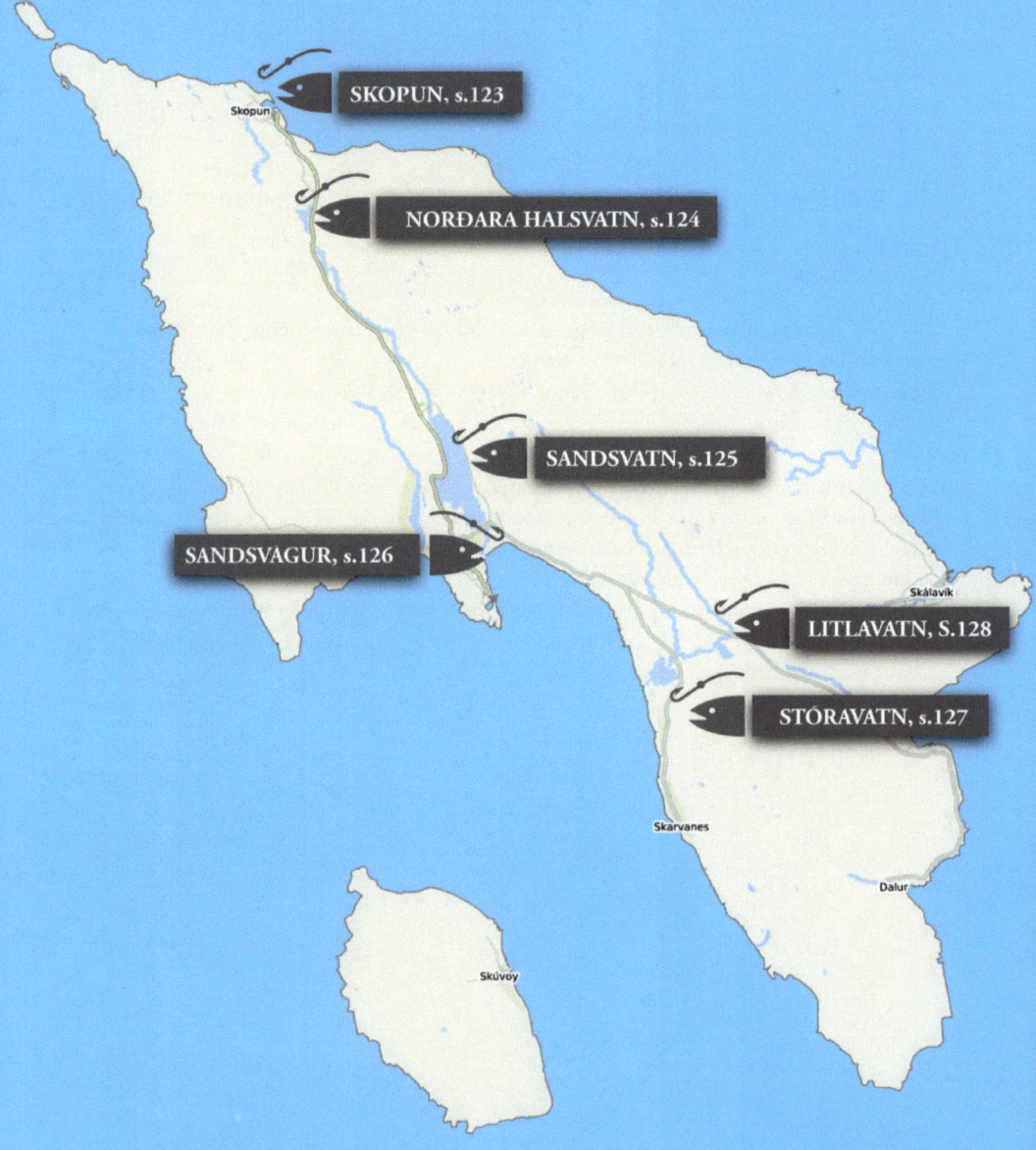

Real Estate Poker on the Sheep Islands

Until the end of 2023, the only way to get to Sandoy was by ferry.
Thanks to this, the clocks on Sandoy ran refreshingly slower and young and old were still wonderfully relaxed. However, what seemed like a romantic sea trip from one idyllic island to the other for us tourists was, for the residents of Sandoy, quite a time-consuming undertaking to get to Tórshavn every day for work, school or shopping.

But since the Faroe Islands have been drilling immense tunnels under the North Atlantic from one large island to the other in the last few decades, very "nonchalantly" and accompanied by worldwide attention, they could not owe the residents of Sandoy anything and also connected - as soon as the budget allowed it – their island within the national road network.

When rumors of the construction of a tunnel began to circulate, smart Faroese quickly bought years before properties on Sandoy or even sold their homes on Streymoy in order to put down new roots on Sandoy resulting at a profit.
After the tunnel was built, a car journey to Torshavn was only 10 minutes instead of 45 minutes by ferry and you can now get to the capital faster than from most other places on Streymoy

Pier Fishing in Skopun

An easily accessible pier fishing spot that promises some success can be found on the quay opposite the former ferry terminal – it's a popular insider tip.
Two fish factories dispose of their "leftovers" in the sea here, making it another spot where birds and fish flock together to feast.

Telltale signs such as fish blood are evidence of colleagues who were there before you – the Faroe Islands aren't known as "the paradise for fishing" for nothing.
You'll discover that for yourself once more here.
Stay towards the right side when casting your line so that you don't lose your set-up in the underwater vegetation.

The Norðara Hálsavatn

Leaving the ferry and heading south towards the blessed waters of Sandoy the expectant angler passes lake Norðara Hálsavatn right hand side. It is easily overlooked and just as easily ignored – a mistake that happened to the author many times. Strange though, because the wildly romantic fishermen's shed (although silent and deserted today) bears witness that these waters have once been the centre of attention for anglers of days gone by.

Having seen many Faroese fishing legends making subtle hints with their hand over their mouths that had something to do with capital brown trouts it was high time to give that lake a try.

To be quite honest: they are hard to see. But there is no chance they resist trained eyes, a tempting fly and a (long) cast well done. And it so happened that there was this rod-bending fight with this most impressive brown trout, an encounter that should make every angler's heart skip a beat.

By the way: be prepared to be cheered from passing drivers. They will applaud your skills, and also the fact that they would have overlooked the lake just like you.

Three times Three: the Propitious Sandsvatn

After Leitisvatn and Fjallavatn on Vágar, Sandsvatn *(see picture on page 119)* is the third-largest lake on the Faroe Islands.
Although it is, in stark contrast to the others, only five metres deep, the brown trout it serves up are larger on average. They grow to a length of around 32 centimetres and live to an age of six years. Their main source of food is larvae and zooplankton.

But Sandsvatn is especially interesting because you'll also come across large specimens of Salmo trutta trutta and natural populations of Salmo salar in its waters.
They climb up via a connection with Sandsvágur to the south.
The sea trout love to move back and forth between the sea and the lakes.

It's easy to fish here from all sides so you can set up in accordance with the prevailing wind direction.
This third-largest lake offers three glorious fish salmonids and is consequently a dream come true for any fisherman.

Sandsvágur, a picture-perfect beach

When great Faroese fishermen talk about Sandsvágur, the beach by Sandur, their eyes begin to sparkle.
And not just because of the wonderful dunes there, which create true holiday feelings like: "sun, sand, sea, and salty kisses".

No – they talk of course about the many sea trout whose bodies dazzle in the backlight as they splash in the rolling wave crests, and the huge specimens such as you'll hardly find elsewhere on these islands.

This beach is also a good example of the boundless freedom and seclusion that the Faroe Islands offer fishermen.
One only rarely sees another anglers on the beach, despite the fact that the sea is teeming with fish. Test it yourself: you've barely cast out a baited hook and you already have a large flatfish pulling on your line – not to mention the chance of catching a large sea trout or a salmon on its way to the lake...

The Siblings, Stóravatn the Great...

You'll reach **Stóravatn** if you take the road towards Skarvanes.
The landscape surrounding the lake is perfectly idyllic and the lake itself serves as a resting stop for many black-legged kittiwakes. On its western slope there is a magnificent waterfall that plunges down 100 metres.

The Author's Story
"I had skirmishes with a brown trout here lasting many years. I knew that it was usually in a weedy spot right where the lake starts, and the first thing I would do when I arrived was to cast at it. It always took the fly at the first cast and yet I never managed to get hold of it. The last time I was there I finally succeeded in catching it. Of course I released it again. Otherwise I'd miss my aquatic friend the next time I came."

...and the little Litlavatn

Litlavatn, whose name translates as "the little lake", lies along the road to Húsavik and Skálavik.
It is the first lake to collect the rain that falls on the mountain standing on the opposite side, the 447-metre Pætursfjall. Its waters then flow into Stóravatn, which lies further below.

Litlavatn is home to larger trout than those that dwell in its bigger brother, which makes it more sensitive to the conduct of fishermen.
Special care and a sense of sustainability should preside when standing on this lakeshore for two reasons.
Firstly, like all lakes on the Faroe Islands, it is private property, which makes every fisherman a tolerated guest. Secondly, its population of fish is only maintained by natural reproduction. But then we all know about the precious commodity with which we're dealing here.

Useful Information and Sightseeing Tips

Húsavík is a picturesque village that is well worth making a detour for. Schoolchildren from Tórshavn are taken on trips here to stay at the school camp.
According to legend, a feisty Faroese lady who came to riches after finding a hoard of gold lived here in the fourteenth century.

There is a good place for breakwater fishing in **Skálavik**, although the village is otherwise rather uninteresting.

The drive to the village of **Dalur** in the east of Sandoy offers wonderful vistas.
And from there it is not much further to the most southerly tip where, with a bit of luck, you can watch puffins from May until the beginning of August.

Highly recommended:
Go **deep sea fishing** with Jóan Peter and his Hvíthamar, a typical Faroese wooden boat made by the master himself *(photo page 157)*. Jóan is a very friendly Faroese and will help you catch lots of fish. Contact via: VisitSandoy, info@visitsandoy.fo or +298 222 078.

Chapter 9

Fishing on Suðuroy, the Wild Isle

Pirate cliffs, Saracens, Vikings – which way is the wind blowing?

They say that funerals on Suðuroy are more joyous events than weddings on the northern island of Borðoy.

Suðuroy is the most southerly of all the Faroe Islands.
Not many fishermen go to the trouble of making the two-hour crossing with the modern Smyril ferry, which is a shame because Suðuroy rewards with a journey into the Faroese past.

Saracens landed here in the seventeenth century and abducted 30 people.
During a second raid, however, their ship was shattered on the rocks and a number of the invaders had to be buried in "Turkish graves".
Others, it is true, left dark-haired, brown-eyed descendants among the island's otherwise fair-skinned and blue-eyed population.
Also interesting are the stories about those fearless islanders who still wrapped their feet in lambskin and wore long pigtails like their Viking forefathers – and this at a time when the Waltz was being danced in Vienna and the Eiffel Tower was already dominating the Paris skyline.

But have no fear: as is the case all over the Faroe Islands, you are a welcome guest.
It's even possible that they'll know you're there before you do.

But if anything is still wild, it is what you as a fisherman can experience on this sea trout island.
Just be sure to take note of which way the wind is blowing...

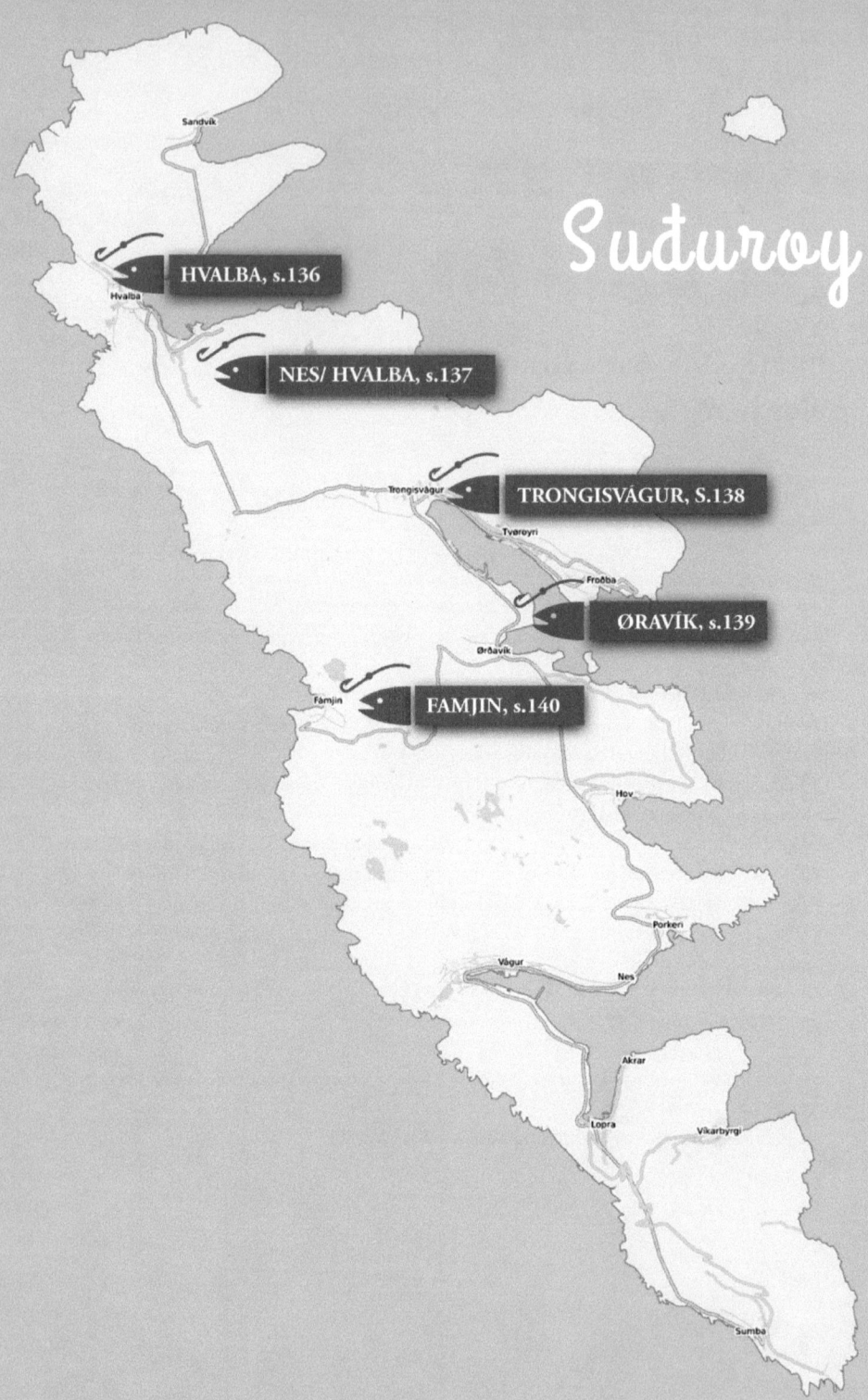

Small; but mighty – in the lake near Hvalba

Heygsvatn lake is very romantic and invitingly located between the heights of the isthmus near the village of Hvalba.
It serves as a well-kept local recreation area and you can often see walkers or locals doing short trips in their car around the lake.

If you want to take it easy and take a few hours off between jumping trout; then you are right here.

In Heygsvatn there are tons - it should be better said - an abundance of brown trout. Due to the numerous occurrences, these are rather small in growth; but are mostly having the minimum size to be keepers.

Nesvegur/Hvalba - Ready for Hollywood

Hvalba makes the hearts of fishermen beat faster, and not just because of the magnificent sea trout.
This village pulsates with the vitality of a colourful history – or material for a Hollywood film: Hvalba was once the largest village on Suduroy.
In 1629, Turkish pirates landed with three ships, killed a few of the residents and took 30 women and children to be sold into slavery. They never returned.
The islands also suffered raids by pirates from Ottoman and North African countries.
These attacks only came to an end when the Danes organised permanent patrols to protect the population.

The only coal mine on the Faroe Islands is located in Hvalba. It was opened in 1770 and it is still in operation today.

The Sea Trouts of Trongisvágur

The Stórá flows into the Trongisvágsfjørður bay between Trongisvágur and Tvøroyri and is very close to where the Smyril ferry arrives.
Both the Stórá and the bay are excellent and easily accessible spots for sea trout fishing.

In the bay you can wade quite far out and look for the fish.
In order to fish in the Stórá, there should have been – like so often on the Faroe Islands – a lot of rainfall beforehand.

A tip from the author: the best time for fishing is once again when the tide is at its highest. Best when there is a new or full moon and if this happens in the hours around sunset.

The bay near **Hov** is also a very good area for sea trout fishing.
Just try it out.

In the neighborhood of Hov is the village of **Porkeri**, which has developed into a Mecca for German deep-sea anglers and real jack-tars in recent years. There you can rent boats from the locals and sail out for fishing on your own risk. It is not without reason that the Faroese fisheries authorities are watching what is happening there with eagle eyes; after all, these going-ons had led to a maximum limit being imposed on the export of fish.

Øravik: Sleepy yet Sprightly

The Author's Story:

"The last time I arrived here I noticed a lot of jumping fish.
I waited until high tide at around midnight, when the fish came in swarms right up to within a metre of the shoreline.
You could almost literally feel their eagerness for prey as they hunted small fish in the whole bay around me.
There were swarms of 50 to 60 trout of all sizes. You only needed to cast with care at the looting fish and you made contact almost every time.
And yet after around three hours the fish's heightened activity finished just as abruptly as it had started.
As ever when fishing, it is a matter of being in the right place at the right time."

Fámjin in the Wild West

When the westerly wind is not blowing, it is worth having a try at the picturesque village of Fámjin. There are many sea trout in good sizes in the whole bay.

The languorous village lies in the west, embedded between high mountains, and it receives the few visitors with a magnificent scenery.
The Merkið, the first ever Faroese flag that was mentioned in the first chapter, hangs in this church.

To the north of Fámjin lies the lake of Kirkjuvatn. It too is a beautiful destination if you have the time. Unfortunately there doesn't seem to be much fish in it.

Useful Information and Sightseeing Tips

The picture shows **Lítla Dímun,** an island on which sheep are left to graze. Once a year, daring men undertake a hazardous mission to abseil the sheep down into boats on their way to slaughter. The meat of these sheep is considered to be particularly delicious.

There is just the one farm on the island of **Stóra Dímun.** It is reached and supplied by helicopter.

If possible, try to take the former country roads - before the tunnel construction - when driving south. They reveal **spectacular panoramas** to you.

Don't miss out - a trip to the **Akraberg lighthouse** at the very southernmost point of the Faroe Islands. You can even receive the Shetland Islands radio station here!

The journey to Suduroy is hardly worth it for just a day's stay, when you like to go fishing.
You should plan for at least a two- or three-night stay.
Just for a sightseeing trip you can do it on one day only. Crossings with the **Smyril Line ferry**. Departure times can be found on ssl.fo.

Chapter 10

Fishing on Vágar, the Nondescript Isle

Unspectacular only at first glance!

In view of the grandeur of the Faroe Islands, you have to remind yourself every once in a while not to overlook the smaller treasures.
Vágar – a name familiar to those travelling here by air – is far more than just the gateway to the Faroe Islands.
The views to the northwest of the villages of Bøur or Gásadalur on the west of the island will stay with you forever.

And the two lakes, Leitisvatn and Fjallavatn, have the potential to create some lasting holiday memories.

Vágar

Leitisvatn - the Giant of Many Faces

At a length of six kilometres and width of 800 metres, Leitisvatn, also known as Sørvágsvatn, is the largest lake on the Faroe Islands. At a depth of 59 metres, it is also the deepest.
It is not directly connected to the sea, so its waters flow via the Bøsdalafossur into the North Atlantic. A very popular panorama among photography enthusiasts.

Not far from the Bøsdalafossur stands the Trælanípa, the Faroese word for "the slave cliff" – a sad story. In the dim and distant past, servants who were no longer able to work, and as a result could not be supported, were thrown off to their deaths.

English seaplanes landed here during the Second World War until the first runway was built, which later became the airport we know today. Leitisvatn is one of the few lakes where fishing is allowed by boat, so it is now home to numerous private boats. It has great potential for fish.

A Moment's Pause: the Spellbinding Fjallavatn

Time for a spot of philosophy: the spectacular Fjallavatn is not hard to reach. Once you've passed the village of Vatnsoyrar you can park your car and walk the remaining 1.2 miles to the southerly point of the lake. The water of the Fjallavatn is crystal clear and its shores are flat and pleasantly soft. It's quite understandable that the Faroese government has made the whole of the surrounding landscape into one of the few nature conservation areas. On the western shore lies the abandoned village of Vikar. All the men of the village died at sea and the women and children had to give up the village and head towards the city. The waters of the Fjallavatn flow back into the Atlantic via the Reipsá in the north – and thus the circle of life closes again.

Sightseeing Tips

You should certainly make a trip towards the northeast to visit the charming village of **Bøur** *(or Bø)* and its picturesque cemetery.
In Bøur is a family living, who are selling beautiful sheep furs.
Contact via their website: faroesheep.com

A favourite subject matter of photographers lies just a little further on: the village of **Gásadalur** with its unique waterfall.

When you catch a glimpse of the rocky islands of **Tindhólmur** and **Gáshólmur**, which are just off the shore of the island of Mykines, you'll understand why they call the Faroe Islands the most beautiful island nation in the world.

If time allows, take a trip to the bird island of **Mykines**, one of the last havens for many seabirds who come here to breed.

Chapter 11

Ship ahoy!

On the high seas, where men are still men.

Sea fishing in Faroese waters is an experience.
The fishing grounds are rich, there is a huge variety of species and the sea is rough – muscle power still counts for something.

And yet they interact with nature with sensitivity here:
the Ministry for Fisheries and Agriculture is strict in upholding sustainability regulations within the 200-mile fisheries zone.
The law also stipulates that at least two-thirds of all crew on board the fleets admitted into the Faroe Islands must be Faroese.

You can't simply sail out to sea and start fishing. Large areas of the seabed around the Faroe Islands consist of coral reef, which are important spawning grounds.
They are closed to any kind of fishing at certain times, in some zones even the whole year round. Trawlers may only fish 40% of the area around the Faroe Plateau from a depth of 200 metres, the Plateau itself is proscribed all year round, as are a number of areas within the 12-mile zone, with the exception of smaller boats for flatfish in summer.

The Four Ws : who, what, when, where …
… to go deep sea fishing

Although the pillars of the archipelago are based on catching pelagic fish and aquaculture, no infrastructure worth mentioning was built up so far for deep sea fishing for tourists.
In every Faroese family, the father, brother-in-law or brother has a little boat with which one goes fishing for cod or halibut when the conditions are favorable.
But you can hardly find skippers who go out to sea as a full-time job with interested anglers.
However, smart Faroese have discovered an additional source of income and are offering their small boats for hire.

Since such providers are subject to frequent changes; this book cannot be a constant source of information.
On the website of the tourist authority there is a summary of the currently valid offers:
Information on: visitfaroeislands.com
Another recommendable site is: boat.fo

Side Note: Not all that flutters is fish

A little warning at this point:
beware of exaggerated euphoria when sea fishing!
Faroese waters may be rich in fish – but not all that flutters is fish by any means.
One overeager fisherman had to learn that lesson the hard way. Having travelled a long way, he cast his line into the water on the first day of his holiday during a trip out to sea.
Feeling something tugging at his line, he was overjoyed to think that Saint Peter, the patron saint of fishermen, was on his side and that the journey would pay off so quickly.
He reeled and reeled, it was just a small one. But what hung on the hook was something quite unexpected: an original Faroese Holed Ribbed Brown – a woollen sock.
Such achievements should also be honoured – the Faroese sea is so clean that this sock is a far rarer catch than any cod.
So: chin up!

Foto of Faroese fish with courtesy of Ingi Sørensen

Chapter 13

Faroese Food Culture

Or how to survive in the North Atlantic

Fulmars, lamb, whale and fish: Faroese cuisine is primal – and is well on its way to being haute cuisine.

Jóan Pauli Joensen is Rector of the University of Tórshavn in the Faroese capital, and he tells me that when he was at school, whale hunting days were big feast days. Hungry schoolchildren went home at lunchtime filled with the thrill of anticipation. Then, back in the classroom, they would all fall asleep within the first 15 minutes of the next lesson. At home they had been given their first substantial meal for a long time. Having said that, Joensen doesn't exactly look like someone who was starved as a child. The portly, round bear of a man looks rather more like a retired football manager than the most important living academic of the Faroe Islands. And yet he speaks of the conditions that have made survival on this part of the earth so difficult since man first set foot upon it.

Hardly anything that is edible or nutritious grows in the barrenness of this weather-battered island archipelago in the middle of the North Atlantic: no grains, no fruit and almost no vegetables. So from where do they get their protein, their vitamins and their minerals?

They get them from the sheep that graze on the rocky landscape, from the birds in the air and from the diversity of life that inhabits the sea, which has always determined life and death here.

However, one stereotype about the Faroe Islands must be countered: despite all the adversities, Faroese cuisine is by no means dull. They make whatever they manage to wring out of the barrenness into a tasty meal.

So much so, in fact, that a movement has been developing recently towards star-quality cuisine based on traditional ingredients.

SHAKEN, NOT STIRRED

The four original cornerstones of Faroese cuisine are mutton, fish, fulmar and pilot whale. Each ingredient has something in common: just as difficult as the acquisition of food was its preservation. There was no electricity until the 1950s, and even then it was only available in urban areas, meaning that keeping food fresh in refrigerators and freezers was not an option. Curing was not a viable alternative because cooking salt, like many other things on the Faroe Islands, was a scarce and therefore expensive commodity. One thing they had always had enough of, however, was air – which is high in salt and sterile, and therefore ideal for air-drying. To this day, a drying house stands next to every house, through whose loose timber walls the wind blows and, together with the fermentation of the meat hanging within, preserves the meat, as well as producing an intense flavour effect. In a nutshell, Faroese preparation of meat means "shaken, not stirred". Sheep play the most important role in the nutritional plan: it's not just coincidence that the name "Faroe" translates as "Sheep Islands". After all, these livestock were said to be the first settlers on the islands and they have remained an unofficial national symbol that one comes across everywhere – from beer adverts to the national costume. In the past, each family would have owned a small flock but now the occupation of the shepherd has become professionalised. Oli Olsen is a shepherd who owns an impressive 130 animals. They are selected for slaughter in October each year and the rule of thumb is: the older they are, the better they taste. As a basic principle, each part of the sheep is used. Heads are put in a broth; cleaned and filled intestines are made into "sperdil", a kind of sausage; the cleaned and hung dried fat is made into "garnatolg", which is a cooking ingredient unique to the Faroe Islands and is an acquired taste. The vast majority, however, is taken to the drying houses in manageable pieces. A distinction is made between three stages at which the mutton is eaten: either fresh after slaughter; as "raest", which means fermented, which takes around 4 weeks; or as the infamous "skerpikjøt", dried, a process that takes six months and that is reserved for only the best cuts of meat. "If the back has a green tinge, the aroma is just right", says Olsen pointing to a few appetising pieces that are glowing red-green. The taste of the dried sheep could be described as harsh and tangy; its aroma is all-pervading and can stay in your clothes and apartment for weeks after preparation.

And yet there are subtle differences between the flavours. It might sound fanciful but various characteristics can be distinguished in the kitchen-crippling odours. What's more, dried mutton legs are comparable to a premium wine. This is because factors such as grassland, flock heredity, age and, of course, the farmer are just as decisive for "skerpikjøt" as the vineyard, grape variety, year and the winemaker are for a good drop of wine. Even Italian gourmets are now interested in Faroese methods of salt-air-drying, Olsen reveals with a smirk. It is said that they have already sent a few test hams up north.

NEW NORDIC KITCHEN

One for whom this topic has nothing to do with fun but rather with his professional honour is master chef Leif Sørensen. High above the rooftops of the capital he used to serve discerning menus at the gourmet restaurant of the Hotel Føroyar. And was the pioneer for all fallwing top chefs. In doing so he drew from the bounty of the natural world that surrounds him. Scallops with crab foam, fish consommé with green mussels and lobster grissini or lamb on cucumber purée are only a few examples of what can be conjured out of Faroese produce without overtaxing the taste buds of the sensitive foodie. Nevertheless, Sørensen's vision was a different one. Together with eleven other master chefs from all over Scandinavia, among them René Redzepi, head chef at the Michelin-starred restaurant Noma in Copenhagen, Sørensen signed a manifesto for the establishment of a new culinary movement, the New Nordic Kitchen, in 2004. Their focus is the modern presentation of traditional Nordic cuisine. Not as a Scandinavian mishmash, however, but with a clear regional, seasonal and restrictive focus. What arrives on your plate is what has always been served in the country, only presented in a smart, contemporary way. No easy task. Sørensen explained the concept: "People used to eat a slice of bread with fish and mutton fat in the mornings, and in the evenings some meat and fat, sometimes just fat or just fish. The people were short and very broad. I'm interested in looking for ways to transform this unbalanced diet into modern high cuisine." It was a challenge he was ready to face. Traditional Faroese food has never been offered on restaurant menus because it was considered to be an essential survival element like drinking water. If you were going to pay for eating out, you would not choose to pay for something so unexceptional. According to Sørensen, it is only in the last few years that a new self-confidence has developed, and with it an identification with original Faroese cooking and its various elements. And that's exactly what he sticked to. He intuitively developed recipes for skerpikjøt with lobster burritos, created avant-garde combinations out of "turrur fisk", from consommé to sauce to foam. It's hard to avoid turrur fisk on the Faroe Islands since it has always been one of the basic foods consumed here. Fresh cod is hung headless after it's caught and is either eaten fermented (reastur), a very pungent experience, or it's consumed later as "turrur", dried fish. Even though it's brittle like wood fibre, the flesh of the fish still contains all of the aroma and nutritional goodness. Like a biologist, Sørensen wandered through nature on the lookout for plants that might have been used by man in the mists of the past. He found thirty, ten of which he had either already used or had identified as being usable. Among them were cress and lettuce types, as well as angelica and rhubarb, all of which are typical for the Faroe Islands – in contrast to the potato, which was practically unknown here until the nineteenth century. There is one ingredient, however, towards which the star chef always took a sceptical stance: "Whale meat may play an important role in our culture but the debate surrounding it is too big for whale to be considered an elegant food." That may be the case for haute cuisine, although a different opinion dominates among the general population. Regrettably, Sørensen changed his professional location and left the Hotel Føroyar, but not without leaving a considerable gastronomic trace of Tórshavn on European haute cuisine.

Flying Delicacies

But it's not just that which swims or grazes on the cliffs that can top off a good meal, but also that which flies above.
Three species of seabird are to be found in traditional Faroese cuisine: the guillemot, the comical puffin and the fulmar, which resembles a seagull, although in the case of the latter it is the young birds that have not yet learned to fly that are considered the most delicious.
Fulmars can also be dried, of course, but even the most hardened of Faroese palates prefers them fresh, whether stewed or roasted, because when cooked this way the oily outer layer of fatty armour is dissolved, improving the taste considerably. In the past they also used to eat the eggs, which had to be collected from the cliffs.
But if you know the Faroese landscape, its majesty and enormity, indeed the hyperdimensionality, you will understand that rock climbing is something of a suicide mission that only the bravest dare to undertake. These days it's better to just go to the shop to buy your eggs.
Faroese cuisine is certainly among those national cuisines that have stayed closest to their origins and is, due to its singularities, one of the most recognisable.
Be it Jóan Pauli Joensen's scientific works, Leif Sørensen's advance into elite cuisine or Oli Olsen's grass-roots sheep- rearing work – they all agree that guests in this country rarely react the same to the unique culinary experience it offers.
One thing is sure: Faroese specialities are like fresh oysters.
You try the first one to see if it tastes good. The second because it tastes good.

Recommended restaurant for traditional Faroe cuisine:
RÆST, Gongin 8, Tórshavn, Tel 411 300

Chapter 14

The Pilot Whale Hunt or „Grindadráp"

A Controversial Topic

There is hardly a food tradition today that is as embroiled in controversy as the consumption of whale meat and hunting pilot whales, the "Grindadráp".

The "Grindadráp" is a central element of Faroese culinary unity.
It is also a deep-seated part of Faroese cultural history. In other words: whale hunting is part of the food tradition and of social life here.

That said, there are weighty arguments put forward by animal rights activists who are opposed to this tradition.

If you approach this topic as an outsider, you owe it to the host country to do so from a neutral perspective.

The fact is that during the times of the Danish monopoly on trade, a supply ship only came by once a year and after that they had to wait another twelve months for more Danish goods. You could only survive if you worked hard and lived off what the barrenness of the islands yielded. The pilot whales were an important source of calories. In good summers, schools of them would repeatedly lose their way and end up in Faroese bays. Their lard in particular was vital in securing the survival of the residents from childhood until old age. Did the meat contain specific substances, an unusual nutritional make-up? Jóan Pauli Joensen of the University of Tórshavn has been researching the subject of whale hunting intensively, but rather than producing complicated tables displaying research results, his explanation for why the whale was so important is a simple one: "Because there was plenty of it." As soon as pilot whales were sighted, calls of "Grindabod!" would resound and the battle between man and animal would begin, a battle that has not changed to this day.

In contrast to other nations, whale hunting was never commercialised on the Faroe Islands and no modern hunting technology was developed. Men wade into the bay with knives as they always have done, carry out an archaic, ritualised slaughter and return with their haul. This is then distributed among the collective according to age-old principles. Everyone has a right to partake of the whale. As a result, the pilot whale cannot be bought in shops and can only rarely be ordered in a restaurant – not because it is banned. The only thing is, it's a basic food, just like fish. You either have it or you don't, and if you don't, you'd better hope that someone will be kind enough to give you some. Furthermore, only a few specimens are caught per year. Hunting the pilot whale is purely a matter of subsistence.

Deep in their hearts the Faroese are very fond of their tradition and are extremely reluctant to give it up. Even when they move abroad. The Faroese father-in-law of the former Danish Prime Minister Anders Fogh Rasmussen caused a stir in the capital of his new hometown with the following anecdote. He bought a small, young, one-metre-long whale at Copenhagen harbour, threw it valiantly over his shoulder and cycled home with it through the traffic, whistling all the while. Joenson laughs as he tells this story: "My imagination couldn't make up Faroese reality."

This tradition has now come under fire from critics.

One of the topics most often debated is the question regarding how endangered the pilot whale really is. The method of killing is also controversial because it is very bloody and disturbing for those who witness it. No one is dependent on whale as a source of food any longer. And finally, it is surely chilling to kill such an intelligent species with such distinctive social behaviours.

But the strongest argument is surely the fact that whale meat has now even become an unhealthy option for humans. The oceans are polluted. The whale is at the end of the aquatic food chain, with the result that whale meat becomes contaminated with environmental poisons. There are also groups on the Faroe Islands who are campaigning for an end to whale hunting because of the damage it does to the country's image.

A Fisherman's Cornucopia

A SUMMARY ABOUT SPORTFISHING ON THE FAROE ISLANDS

Of one thing we can be sure:
When there is ONE country that has a saying "Small, but OH!" then it has to be the Faroes. The average recreational angler may consider these islands somewhat isolated geographically, perhaps to be compared with the Shetland Islands, or some Danish islands in the Baltic, but this impression is quickly revised once you stand on the shore with a fishing rod in your hand.

You have to experience the Faroes for yourself, if only because it is difficult to get hold of detailed information in advance of your trip. In fact, there is very little literature on the topic of sports fishing on the Faroes. Yes, there are some blogs and the occasional travel tip via testimonials, but these are mostly just 'snapshot' impressions and are not really based on years of local knowledge. Very much in contrast are the publications of Mauritia Kirchner, herself a passionate fly fisherman. She has lived on the Faroes, her 'adopted home' for almost 15 years and is regarded as a pioneer in her chosen field. She has a great affection for the country and works informally to engage with travellers who are interested in angling. She has already published numerous magazine articles, a travel guide especially for those interested in fishing, and was a guest, and a consultant on several television documentaries. Here she presents some key facts about fishing on the "Islands of Sheep".

A paradise - not only for anglers

The first word that comes to mind about the Faroes is 'harsh'. This is closely followed by 'overwhelming'. On the map, the Faroes are made up of 18 islands, with no point being further from the sea than five kilometres. 'Water' is, therefore, the country's most dominant element, and this transforms the Faroes into a paradise, not only for anglers but especially for them.

Due to its geographical location between Scotland and Iceland, and the fact that it represents a mix of the cold polar water and the warm gulf stream, the water around the Faroes is one of the most fish-rich of the North Atlantic. But there is also something special on offer 'ashore'. You have to imagine the Faroes as the tips of a mountain range that have appeared out of the ocean. They are green, and they are majestic. The terrain drops directly into the sea to a depth of up to 882 metres. Rivers are, in general, only channels for run-off water, which after periods of little rain, all but dry up. However, the archipelago has abundant rainfall, so the impressive waterfalls are refilled continuously.

Possibilities for sports fishing on the Faroes are almost limitless. Anglers have the choice of deep-sea fishing, fishing from a jetty, breakwater or beach, or fishing in one of the many lakes. There is an absolute wealth of fish that are genetically pure. The sport is accessible to beginners and also full of challenges for professionals. Today you could choose to fish in a lake for salmon, tomorrow for cod at sea, the day after for sea trout at the shores. Here, fishing is all about how the mood takes you, provided the weather is right. So now it's time to say a few words about the weather.

In actual fact, the climate on the Faroes is ideal for anglers. Due to the gulf stream, the winter is relatively mild (3°C on average), and situated in the north means it has fresh, windy summers (11°C on average). At midsummer in June, it is light for 24 hours, and that means 24 hours for fishing. And the wind takes care of the rest. A stiff breeze can also be helpful for those who lack experience in casting. But there are some things to note. The climate is rough, and nature is primal. Life is in direct contact with the elements earth and water. That means you have to respect them and be ready for anything. When the sun shines at 10 a.m., you may well be happy an hour later that you brought your rain jacket.

However, those who know how to read nature, and use it correctly can experience unforgettable hours on the water. And as the saying goes: There is no wrong weather for fishing, only the wrong clothes.

FISHING ON THE FAROES: The 'Where' and especially, the 'What'

FRESHWATER - The 'Where'
Water is present on the Faroes in many diverse forms and speeds, some significant, others less so. Fishing in the rivers, however, plays practically no role. The geological characteristics of the islands mean the rivers only accommodate runoff rainwater. Fishing in the small mountain lakes, however, is a multifaceted pleasure. These natural jewels can be found on each of the islands and sometimes represent real treasure both regarding the landscape, and the underwater world. Larger lakes are located on the islands of Vagar, Eysturoy and Sandoy.

FRESHWATER – The 'What'
Non-predatory fish, such as carps or others like pike do not occur naturally on the Faroe Islands. From time to time it is possible to catch a small type of arctic char.
It is in this water that you fish for brown trout, sea trout and in summer time for salmon.

To set the scene: The Faroes are not a classic salmon territory. There are only two lakes that rate as successful for **salmon** fishing, the Leynavatn with its two Mjóuvøtn lakes further upstream, and the lake in Saksun. As a general rule, these lakes yield up to 10 large salmon per day. The season is mostly from the end of July to mid-October. Much credit for this must go to the Faroes Fishing Association with its around 300 members, who have been very engaged over past decades in rearing and stocking Atlantic salmon, which they do with considerable expertise and enthusiasm.

In principle, the genetics of the Icelandic salmon have been adopted, although in recent years some 'escapees' from aquaculture cages have joined the wild salmon population.

Sea trout are the real treasure of the Faroes. You find them everywhere and in large numbers, and there is no set season. However, fish over 60cm are seldom caught. They can be found in numbers where fresh water runs into the sea in specific radii to the coast, where they appear on the tides in large quantities or shoals.

Sea trout mostly feed on sand eels or crustaceans and therefore have rich red meat. They migrate to freshwater areas to spawn during the winter months, and they also like to alternate between fresh and salt water areas throughout the year. Important to note: it is not permitted to take fish under 30cm, and in this case, 'catch and release' is to be practised. Faroese anglers are very keen to protect and keep this species.

Apart from sea trout, the **brown trout** represents one of the real treasures of the islands. They are present in all the lakes and appear in different sizes and colours. Here one should dismiss one commonly held view: the bigger the lake, the bigger the fish - right? No, wrong. The opposite often applies. It is probably wiser to take note that if the water is relatively inaccessible, there is likely to be an abundance of fish. It is also important to be aware of the fact that in the Faroe Islands, in contrast to the lakes in continental Europe that have generous amounts of fish food, brown trout grow very slowly in the nutrient-poor lochs, and a fish between 30-40cm represents a Methuselah who deserves to be released. This is especially the case because there is no restocking of this wild species of self-reproducing fish.

Important to know: Every lake in the Faroe Islands is privately owned. Fishing is mostly tolerated, and respectful behaviour is required. To keep it this way, every guest should ask permission before they begin their activities.

For the Leynavatn, Mjóuvøtn and Saksunartvatn lakes, which are leased by the Faroese Fishing Association, it is necessary to buy a fishing license.

Find out about the current valid times to fish, the regulations and the contact points for acquiring a fishing license on the Fishing Association's website www.laks.fo

SALTWATER – The 'Where' and 'What'
As we mentioned in the beginning, there is no point on the Faroes that is further than five kilometres from the ocean, and that means if you plan to fish in the sea, just follow the island map. It is possible to fish for sea trout and flatfish in all bays and inlets, ideally with sandy soil. It is possible to fill whole tubs with pollack when fishing from jetties and breakwaters. Deep-sea fishing yields cod, pollack, ling, ocean perch, flatfish and mackerel, and it is not uncommon to catch up to 14 varieties of fish in a single day. There are large areas of coral reef on the seabed surrounding the Faroes, and these are important spawning grounds.

Deep-sea fishing in the North Atlantic is a real adventure. The deep, ice-cold water, the sometimes-raw conditions, and the rough seas all require seaworthiness and a little daring, but the reward is impressive. The fishing grounds are abundant, and a successful catch is practically guaranteed. And when back home, you can also entertain the landlubbers with a fascinating description of your fishing trip.

Meanwhile, a word of warning: As a newcomer or tourist you should never go out to sea alone to fish.

What are you waiting for?
If the Faroes are presently just an unknown destination on your travel map, if you just know they are somewhere far in the north and have perhaps heard a passing reference regarding football, it is time to discover them for yourself.
The Faroes are breathtakingly beautiful, hospitable, modern, and at the same time such a primal land that it is certainly one of the world's last paradises – and not just for anglers.

www.ingramcontent.com/pod-product-compliance
Lightning Source LLC
Chambersburg PA
CBHW040015240426
43664CB00036B/3